On Keats's Practice ar
of Responsibili ̌y

G. Douglas Atkins

On Keats's Practice and Poetics of Responsibility

Beauty and Truth in the Major Poems

palgrave
macmillan

G. Douglas Atkins
Greenville
South Carolina
USA

ISBN 978-3-319-82994-4 ISBN 978-3-319-44144-3 (eBook)
DOI 10.1007/978-3-319-44144-3

Cover illustration: Pattern adapted from an Indian cotton print produced in the 19th century

Printed on acid-free paper

This Palgrave Macmillan imprint is published by Springer Nature
The registered company is Springer International Publishing AG
The registered company address is: Gewerbestrasse 11, 6330 Cham, Switzerland

It is a strange habit of wise humanity to speak in enigmas only, so that the highest truths and usefullest laws must be hunted for through whole picture-galleries of dreams, which to the vulgar seem dreams only.

—John Ruskin

For Rebecca

PREFACE

For a man who died so young—just 25, about one-third of my age—John Keats was remarkably sensitive, sympathetic, capacious, and warm-hearted. Reading his letters anew, I feel even more closely and surely the presence of another human being than when I read anyone else's writing—that the letters are, of course, in the present tense no doubt contributes to this effect. Perhaps for the first time, in any case, I begin here actually to *read* the letters, some of them (at least) as essayistic and dramatic. Reading Keats, prose and verse alike, is an adventure in what it means to be a fully functioning human: an unblinkered recognition of the world, its evil, and its suffering that does not manage to eclipse the beauty that "is a joy for ever." Keats is no more a poet for our benighted time than for any other. His life was so difficult, his advantages few, and even so—or, perhaps, because of that—he found beauty enough to sustain him, and us, in the world, whose truth, he never forgets or allows us to, is painful, full of suffering, and too often tragic. I can think of no better word to describe John Keats, warts and all, than "responsible."

His whole writing career extends only from 1814 to mid-1820, barely 6 years, but these are wondrous. In those years, writing makes all the difference; it is in, through, and by means of the writing, in verse and prose alike, that Keats's ideas developed, with indications of change in point of view. What matters most to apprehension of both continuity and change in the art and understanding alike is *saturation* in the poet's work.

This little book I hope will be taken up, and found readable and useful, by academics, specialists, and non-specialists alike, as well as by the so-called general reader who has heard of Keats and desires an introduction to his poetry that takes seriously the ideas dramatized therein. To borrow a distinction made decades ago by G. Wilson Knight, the book you are holding aligns itself with "interpretation," rather than "criticism." Although I do not subscribe to all of Knight's notions, including the rein he gives to impressions and the imprecision with which he sometimes proceeds, I do think his distinction between these two approaches in the main useful: "The critic," he wrote, "is, and should be, cool and urbane, seeing the poetry he [or she] discusses not with the eyes of a lover but as an object; whereas interpretation deliberately immerses itself in its theme and speaks less from the seats of judgment than from the creative centre." I want to signal, as well, that I see my work as "commentary," rather than "criticism," for I am little interested in (negative) judgment and very much committed to sympathetic engagement with the poet. If I add, this time borrowing from Roland Barthes, that this book may be seen as *a lover's discourse*, I perhaps have shown a penchant for such complex-ifying and perplexing as Keats himself might approve. Whether or not he would approve, I find myself both within and outside the "camp" of the legendary Earl Wasserman, whose *The Finer Tone: Keats' Major Poems*, dating from 1953, remains "the gold standard" for close reading of the verse. I am tempted to say that the tenor of the present book perhaps carries some of that of Wasserman's book, while its texture is markedly different. The form in which I write is essayistic (but the analysis, I hope, is not less scrupulous), and I am much less inclined than Wasserman to find the spiritual around every corner. My "tone" is, then, less "fine," but in that regard, it is closer, I believe, to Keats. So as not to impede readability, I have kept endnotes to a minimum; in the Bibliography, however, I have listed those many books, articles, and essays that I have found most helpful, perhaps especially when I disagree with them. For the sake of convenience, I have referred, except where otherwise noted, to *Selected Poems*, ed. Douglas Bush (Boston, MA: Riverside-Houghton Mifflin, 1959).

With deep and abiding gratitude, I acknowledge my debt to E.D. Hirsch, in whose seminar at the University of Virginia decades ago I first learned to read Keats. Others bear responsibility for so much of the good here (and none of the wrongheaded and inarticulate): I mean Rus Hart, the late Irvin Ehrenpreis, the late Geoffrey Hartman, and Vincent Miller. Once more, I am happy to acknowledge my considerable debt to Pam

LeRow, in the word-processing center back at the University of Kansas, who still comes to my rescue, now Emeritus, in preparing my work for submission in electronic form. And happily and gratefully, I record my continuing debt to, and gratitude for, my children Leslie Atkins Durham and Christopher Douglas Atkins, their spouses Craig and Sharon, and my grandchildren, Kate and Oliver. Finally, there is Rebecca, my Madeline and "a thing of beauty"; I am happy to dedicate this book to her.

CONTENTS

CHAPTER 1

On Reading Keats: Essaying Toward Reader-Responsibility

Abstract Studies of the poet's short, tragic life still dominate the scholarship, but "Reading Keats" has recently become a topic of some interest in the commentary. This book offers a professional-amateur approach, written for specialist and general reader alike, and focusing on Keats's deep sense of responsibility to his readers, the world as he understood it, and the vocation whose burdens he struggled with. The book's point of view is contrasted with that in such recent commentary as that by Jack Stillinger, Susan Wolfson, Stanley Plumly, and Eric G. Wilson.

Keywords Matters of reading Keats · Professional-amateur approach · Poet's responsibility to readers · Earlier commentary

> The readerly act is also the writerly act. And if the critic's writing-up of that identification is also metaphorical, then we can bestow a slightly enriched meaning on Arnold Isenberg's original phrase "sameness of vision." We are all, writer, reader, and rewriter (the critic), engaged in a sameness of vision that is in some ways a *sameness of writing*.
>
> —James Wood, *The Nearest Thing to Life*

The Victorians famously believed that Keats's poems mean "next to nothing," largely void of ideas but full of beautiful pictures. We have come a long way in the intervening 125 years or so. Now it appears—to the ama-teur,

© The Author(s) 2016
G.D. Atkins, *On Keats's Practice and Poetics of Responsibility*,
DOI 10.1007/978-3-319-44144-3_1

anyway, the reader interested in the poetry as poetry—that the pendulum has swung so far in the opposite direction that we seem interested in, or able to deal with, little other than Keats's "ideas." By that is meant either those ideas manifest within the writing itself, or else the results of bringing outside perspectives to bear on the writing, biographical, historical, or theoretical.

This book is different. Because I am an ama-teur, rather than a specialist in Keats or the Romantics, I treat scholarship as a means, not an end. The ideas, in the letters and the poems alike, matter greatly, but my interests lie first in how the verse and the prose work—as writing, that is, not princi-pally as expression of ideas. With Nobel Prize-winning poet Odysseus Elytis, I consider poetry (at least) in terms of the simultaneity that marks the birth of ideas and their expression.[1] Necessarily, therefore, attention focuses on the poems and letters as works of literature, works of art.

The scholarship that appears (to this "outsider") to dominate critical commentary on Keats nowadays honors the *new*—which translates as discovered ideas or imported. A great deal of value attaches to this work (I think immediately, to name but one such writer, Grant Scott, editor of the magisterial "new" edition of the letters and author of the book *The Sculpted Word: Keats, Ekphrasis, and the Visual Arts*). But surely there is room—among the significant number of books on Keats—for a different kind, one that, without reducing or minimizing their importance, does not begin with ideas, or privilege them unduly.

While I write here about Keats's intersection with me, I am interested principally in recording and analyzing the experience of reading both the poems and the letters. Reading them is at once enjoyable, rewarding, and instructive. You both learn from the letters and the poems and derive pleasure by and from reading them carefully, attentively, and responsibly.

Unlike the great majority of commentators on Keats, moreover, I *read* both the verse and the prose. I mean the letters that T.S. Eliot greeted as "certainly the most notable and the most important ever written by any English poet" and that Lionel Trilling later praised as rivaling the poems in distinction. In spite of all, then, my work on Keats may earn the scholarly honorific of *new* in more ways than one. A postscript to my essay on "The Eve of St. Agnes" marks the direction of a possible new interpretation; my readings of the Odes include comparison with T.S. Eliot's treatment of the same subjects; and my account of "Lamia" is entirely new.[2]

As I was struggling to clarify what it is that we need, in general and in respect to Keats (and Eliot) in particular, in other words, and to refine my long-held sense of the inseparability of writing and reading, I came across the endlessly suggestive Mandel Lectures at Brandeis University given by the eminent "practical critic" James Wood, Professor of the Practice of Literary Criticism at Harvard University. Reading *The Nearest Thing to Life*, I felt in the presence, and as if being gifted with the voice, of a writer who quite often says it better (*"il fabbro miglior,"* as Eliot said of Pound).[3] "A lot of the criticism that I admire," writes Wood with the courage of my convictions, "is not especially analytical but is really a kind of passionate redescription."[4] (These words call to my mind the commentary of Andrew Lytle and, differently, William Maxwell,[5] while reminding me of the bruises I still bear from an anonymous reviewer of a recent manuscript of mine, who, declining to recommend publication, thought I said little beyond what any reasonably attentive reader could see and appreciate.) We await an extended argument for "commentary" (rather than "criticism").

Wood continues, in apt words that help to explain and develop his position (and foreshadow mine here):

> The written equivalent of the reading aloud of a poem or a play is a retelling of the literature one is talking about; the good critic has an awareness that criticism means, in part, telling a story about the story you are reading, as De Quincey binds us into the story of his readerly detection [in "On the Knocking at the Gate in *Macbeth*"].[6]

From this point, Wood proceeds to further elaboration, sparking a relation to Geoffrey Hartman while steering clear of anything like "creative criticism" (abjured by Eliot, incidentally, but advocated by Hartman, and recently reprised with modifications by the eminent Shakespearian Graham Holderness):

> I would call this kind of critical retelling a way of writing *through* books, not just about them. This writing-through is often achieved by using the language of metaphor and simile that literature itself uses. It is a recognition that literary criticism is unique because one has the privilege of performing it in the same medium one is describing. [Critics in this mode] are speaking to literature in its own language. This speaking to literature in its own language is indeed the equivalent of a musical or theatrical performance; an act of critique that is at the same time a revoicing.[7]

As powerful a writer as he is, and well-established in both academic and "writerly" circles, James Wood tiptoes around a very tempting notion: he speaks, as we have seen, of criticism as (re)description, and he refers to it as a "writerly act." He appears to resist, however, claiming that it is a rewriting, although at one point he does refer to the critic as "rewriter." Wood resists with good reason, of course, any implication that the critic is on a par with the poet. There should be, in my judgment, no equating of writer and commentator, no claim that the reader *creates* the meaning of the text, being not simply the agent who reveals but he or she who makes that meaning. The death of the author, according to Roland Barthes, is the birth of the reader, an argument traceable, ultimately, to its beginnings in the Protestant Reformation, with its instauration of "the priesthood of all readers." The enfranchised reader is not responsible for textual meaning.

I thus resist the notion that literary commentary is a "rewriting" of the original, calling text. Rewriting often (at least) implies revising, making different, perhaps making better, removing errors and missteps, shaping things anew. If this is what follows from James Wood's astute observations, I would have to part ways. If by "rewriting," we mean "writing again," why not—better, in my estimation—call it putting-in-other-words?

At any rate, the way of reading that I practice, is precisely a *way*, admittedly a point of view, and it opens a reading, rather than closes it. It always insists on the reader's *responsibility*, beginning with obligations to himself or herself of being other than a passive receptacle. Another, primary responsibility is the reader's to the poem and to the poet, with which and with whom she or he is (thus) intersecting. (In the course of this work, we will see, importantly, that this strategy—shall we call it?—mirrors the subject's, that is, Keats's, way of going about the writing of the primary texts.)

In order to pinpoint the character of my own position, I will mention some other approaches that differ from mine. I refer first to that promulgated by Jack Stillinger in his *Reading "The Eve of St. Agnes": The Multiples of Complex Literary Transaction*. The book stems from his controversial earlier article on "The Hoodwinking of Madeline: Skepticism in 'The Eve of St. Agnes,'" which I consider at some length in my chapter below on this poem. From the time of that essay's first publication in 1961, its inclusion 10 years later in his edited collection *"The Hoodwinking of Madeline" and Other Essays on Keats's Poems,* and the publication of the new book in 1999, Stillinger's position changed. But the change more solidly affects his theoretical assumptions than his actual consideration of the one poem. He still, evidently, clings to many of the original sub-arguments: that Madeline is "hoodwinked," that Porphyro is in reality a rapist, that the poem as a whole reflects Keats's considered "skepticism." Over the years, however, Stillinger has come to believe, an advocate of diversity, that there is not *one* reading of such a work, but as many as there are readers: in an affirmation of multi-criticalism, Stillinger thus says that your reading is ok, mine ok too. What would, then, be the practical effect is the inevitability of imposition upon the poem, an outcome that amounts to something other than a *reading*. I mention this later version of Stillinger's approach here since I will concern myself chiefly with his earlier reading in setting up my own arguments below in Chapter 4. As I have stated, my focus is the poems, and to a less extent the letters, and how they work as literary texts: not just what they say but how they say it, what they do (as well as say), and how one part is related to another and to the work as a whole (the issues of hermeneutics). It is a matter, in other words, of architectonics, not biography, even less so memoir or autobiography. Throughout, I work to insure that my writing is governed by my close *reading*, not by theoretical, ideational, or ideological imposition of *a priori* assumptions.

My book differs as well from *Reading John Keats* by Susan J. Wolfson, which appeared as mine was approaching production-stage and which is dedicated to Jack Stillinger. Preliminary attention finds it to be, in any case, a book well worth considering, with rather different interests: evidently, her title represents "reading" as both verb and adjective. *Reading John Keats* provokes us to reflect on what it is to "read, fail to read, misread, reread, read better."

Another matter needs addressing by way of contextualizing my own efforts and situating them among the lively and growing number of books relating the poet, the poems, and the reader. Some of the solid efforts of the past quarter of a century or so might enlist under the general category of "personal criticism," a notion that in the early 1990s I embraced, exemplified, and thus sought to advance, particularly in *Estranging the Familiar: Toward a Revitalized Critical Writing*. While I remain convinced of our need for, and the possibility of, a way of doing literary commentary displaying the reader's engagement with the text and offered in a manner generally essayistic (rather than positivistic, distanced, and even contrarian and antagonistic), I am not drawn to the indiscriminate mixing of commentary and autobiography in once-vibrant feminist criticism and now in the efforts of the uber-prolific Harold Bloom.

Commentators on Keats have been more successful, I believe, than many in bringing the critic *into* the efforts of writing about a poet. For example, Susan Wolfson's aforementioned *Reading John Keats* appears to be an admirable balance of critical analysis and personal and reflective acknowledgment: illuminating without being "objective," low on auto-biography without disengagement or dry-as-dust. The poet Stanley Plumly's intriguing *Posthumous Keats: A Personal Biography* is perhaps even more interesting, although ultimately less satisfying. Something of a curiosity, this book evinces a major issue in all attempts to combine "the personal" with critical analysis and commentary. Plumly may be seen as neatly sidestepping some of the entailed problems by focusing his "perso-nal" considerations on the poet rather than the poems; even so, readers persist in asking about the poetry. More recently, Eric G. Wilson has forged a new and different path in *How to Make a Soul: The Wisdom of John Keats.* The publisher describes it as "an innovative hybrid of biography, memoir, and criticism." Even though the title smacks of the contemporary "self-help" craze, Wilson establishes from the beginning a definite and solid difference. But like Plumly's, Wilson's book generally sacrifices the poem to the poet, perhaps an instance of wisdom not likely learned from the poet.

It is extraordinarily difficult to find a way of marrying the personal/familiar/essayistic and the analytical/critical/"definite article." I have been trying for 25 years or more; and indeed, I know of scarcely any successful attempts, a striking exception being E.B. White's paean to Henry David Thoreau, "A Slight Sound at Evening" (in which, inciden-tally, the self-observing is not so much observed as artfully constructed and rendered dramatically). As to *How to Make a Soul,* Wilson ends up writing a good deal about himself, and a good deal about the man and the poet John Keats. His interest sets him apart, however, from so many of the practitioners of what has been derisively labeled "*moi* criticism," little (self-)indulgence here, as a matter of fact. Wilson proceeds in, through, and by means of his private, individual experience to general-ized, if not always universal, application. It is, then, essayistic, but the self that does the observing too easily becomes the self-observed, and in thus succumbing to the memoiristic pull, Wilson slides over from the familiar type of critical essay to the far more prevalent personal type (the familiar and the personal being the two major kinds of essay).

My preference for the familiar is obvious enough, I reckon—hence, no doubt, my predilections for Dryden, Swift, and Pope, as well as Eliot and

E.B. White: I side with the restrained, but not the distanced, the engaged, but not the (self-)indulgent. Hence, then, the book that you hold focuses on the poems (and to lesser extent, the letters): in other words, on the writing, in prose as well as verse. Of course, Keats is the sort of writer for whom the writing can never fully be separated from the man who wields the pen—nor from the woman or man engaged in reading that writing and then writing about that reading. The situation is, willy-nilly, dramatic, and of the comic variety, not the tragic (like this poet's life). How to respond to "circumstances"—a familiar theme in Keats's letters and one fraught with *personal* weight—is our burden, too.

The temptation to write about Keats the man, rather than the poems, is great, indeed, and I too have felt it, and at times succumbed to the desire. Happily, biographies are plentiful—while, as I have said, literary analyses, particularly close readings, are scarce. The standard biography remains that of Walter Jackson Bate, although others should be noted as certainly worthy of attention and consideration, including those of Aileen Ward, Robert Gittings, and, most recently, and controversially, Nicholas Roe. With prime importance given to close linguistic and structural analysis—to the poems as works of literary *art*—the reader of the present book might expect a good amount of quoting and healthy doses of textual particularities.

A final, related point for me here concerns audience. Again I will cite, as instance of what I am talking about, a recent publisher's review of another submitted manuscript of mine. That anonymous reviewer reports having "struggled throughout the manuscript" with "the question of audience," for, he or she goes on, "my sense is that he [that is, me] is a specialized scholar trying to write a work approachable by generalists, a conflict that results in an unpredictable tone and an uncertain audience." The fact is, of course, that I am not a "specialized scholar," although I have published several books on Eliot (my specialties, insofar as I can even lay claim to any, are in the Restoration and early eighteenth-century British poetry and prose, contemporary criticism and theory, and the essay—I never even had a graduate course in Eliot, nor did I teach him, beyond the sophomore survey, until 2001). I am even further from being a Keats specialist!

Furthermore, the audience I seek and write for is not at all "uncertain"; it is quite certain, as a matter of fact, although my sense of audience obviously differs radically from this reviewer's: there is no reason that I can see that one's audience has to be an either/or in order to be "certain." Indeed, tension does not equate with "conflict." Still, the reviewer ends by claiming, "More importantly, the unevenness has the dual potential to overestimate the knowledge of generalist readers and to condescend to specialists." The commentary stings, all right. I can say, though, that a writer should aim to respect readers, of all sorts, not to condescend to them or to require too little of them, patronizing. I would like to ask more of the generalist reader while reminding the specialist that she or he is not the whole audience but only a part, whose job should include sharing some general and universal interests of other readers. I write, that is to say, for both kinds of readers, at once, committed to the idea that there are not two audiences but one. Just as truth and beauty are one, Keats thought.

NOTES

1. Odyseus Elytis, *Analogies of Light*, ed. Ivar Ivask (Norman: U of Oklahoma P, 1981), 8.
2. See my books *Strategy and Purpose in T.S. Eliot's Major Poems: Language, Hermeneutics, and Ancient Truth in "New Verse"* (New York: Palgrave Macmillan, 2015), and *T.S. Eliot's Christmas Poems: An Essay in Writing-as-Reading and Other "Impossible Unions"* (New York: Palgrave Macmillan, 2014). I am here, though, actually rewriting my own earlier work on Keats: see my *"The Eve of St. Agnes* Reconsidered," *Tennessee Studies in Literature* 18 (1973), 113–32; "A Grander Scheme of Salvation than the Chryst[e]ain Religion": John Keats, a New Religion of Love, and the Hoodwinking of 'The Eve of St. Agnes,'" *Literary Paths to Religious Understanding: Essays on Dryden, Pope, Keats, George Eliot, Joyce, T.S. Eliot, and E.B. White* (New York: Palgrave Macmillan), 43–57. The most astute account of Keats's "religion" remains Ronald A. Sharp, *Keats, Skepticism, and the Religion of Beauty* (Athens: U of Georgia P, 1979).
3. Eliot's dedication to Pound appears first in *Poems 1909–1925* (London: Faber and Gwyer, 1925).
4. James Wood, *The Nearest Thing to Life* (Waltham, MA: Brandeis UP, 2015), 83.
5. I think here of Andrew Lytle, *The Hero with the Private Parts* (Baton Rouge: Louisiana State UP, 1966) and William Maxwell, *The Outermost Dream: Essays and Reviews* (New York: Knopf, 1989).
6. Wood, *Nearest Thing to Life*, 83–84.
7. Wood, 84.

CHAPTER 2

Reading the Letters:
"The vale of Soul-making"

Abstract T.S. Eliot regarded Keats's letters as "certainly the most notable and the most important ever written by any English poet." The famous mini-essays include the passage on the "vale of Soul-making," presented as a more satisfactory "scheme of salvation" than Christianity; for Keats, a world of "circumstances" is necessary for the creation of a soul. This chapter considers the letters in detail, focusing on the character of the writer and the sense of humanity and responsibility the letters embody. The letters are *read*, that is, regarded as poems are and treated as essays (that is, attempts, trials) and understood as more than straightforward expositions of set ideas. Many of the letters, as Eliot said, "are of the finest quality of criticism."

Keyword Letters soul-making · Circumstances reading letters as literature

> ... I began by seeing how man was formed by circumstances—and what are circumstances?—but touchstones of his heart—? And what are touchstones?—but proovings of his hearrt? And what are proovings of his heart but fortifiers or alterers of his nature? And what is his altered nature but his soul?—and what was his soul before it came into the world and had These provings and alterations and perfectionings?—An intelligences—without Identity—and how is this Identity to be made? Through the medium of the Heart? And how is the heart to become this Medium but in a world of Circumstances?
>
> —Letter, 21 April 1819, to George and Georgiana Keats

© The Author(s) 2016
G.D. Atkins, *On Keats's Practice and Poetics of Responsibility*,
DOI 10.1007/978-3-319-44144-3_2

[Y]ou perhaps at one time thought there was such a thing as Worldly Happiness to be arrived at, at certain periods of time marked out—you have of necessity from your disposition been thus led away—I scarcely remember counting upon any Happiness—I look not for it if it be not in the present hour—nothing startles me beyond the Moment.

—Letter of 22 November 1817 to Benjamin Bailey

Dead at 25, John Keats had every reason to doubt the availability of happiness, beyond the isolated, intense moment, that is. He knew loss, pain, and suffering intimately. Born (perhaps) in a livery stable, on Halloween 1795, the son of the head ostler and the daughter of the owner, he was orphaned at 15—his father had died 6 years earlier. His mother succumbed to the tuberculosis that would later take his brother Tom's life and eventually the poet's. Although his grandmother provided a trust fund of around 400,000 pounds (in today's money) for John, Tom, their brother George, and their sister Fanny, John never saw any of it and lived his few remaining years in debt and distress. Partly as a result of his financial condition, John was never able to marry his beloved Fanny Brawne. He apprenticed as an apothecary, and studied as a medical student, receiving his apothecary's license in 1816, which certified him to practice not just as an apothecary but also as a physician and surgeon. John subsequently took up care of his brother Tom, who died of tuberculosis in December 1818; George, meanwhile, married, and he and Georgiana moved to Louisville, Kentucky, where they too died penniless and tubercular. Long suffering from colds, John persevered in his ambition to be a poet, encouraged by Coleridge, Leigh Hunt, and others.[1]

Early on, menaced by lack of money, his own illness, probably including depression, and, among other stresses, his brotherly love for the dying Tom, John Keats felt acutely the burden of both personal and poetic responsibility. Before long, as he launched a poetic career, he knew he was destined soon to die: among the expressions of both knowledge and responsibility stands the example of a sonnet written in late January 1818, which begins, "When I have fears that I may cease to be/Before my pen has glean'd my teeming brain. . . . " The burden of responsibility he felt to poetry existed alongside the poor and often mean-spirited response his poems received, particularly from reviewers. Before he died on 23 February 1821, he published three volumes, which combined sold only around 200 copies: *Poems* (1817), *Endymion* (1818), and *Lamia, Isabella, The Eve of St. Agnes, and Other Poems* (July 1820).[2]

In his lifetime, Keats thus fared little better as a poet than he did as a man. Commentary, such as it was, treated him disrespectfully, and irresponsibly. Dismissal greeted his first book and the dismal reception of his work reached a peak in the representation of him as effete, ascetic, and morally and spiritually weak. It was widely bruited about that the brutally harsh early reviews even led to his early death at 25, barely 3 years after that first book, of which even the publishers were ashamed. His friend Percy Bysshe Shelley famously responded in the poem *Adonais*.

The Quarterly Review ventured this scathing indictment in April 1818, aligning Keats with the "Cockney School," which it said,

> may be defined to consist of the most incongruous ideas in the most uncouth language.... There is hardly a complete couplet enclosing a complete idea in the whole book. He wanders from one subject to another, from the association, not of ideas, but of sounds.[3]

Not to be outdone, *Blackwood's Edinburgh Magazine* offered this personal—and embarrassing—attack:

> To witness the disease of any human understanding, however feeble, is distressing; but the spectacle of an able mind reduced to a state of insanity is, of course, ten times more afflicting. It is with such sorrow as this that we have contemplated the case of Mr. John Keats.... He was bound apprentice some years ago to a worthy apothecary in town. But all has been undone by a sudden attack of the malady.... For some time we were in hopes that he might get off with a violent fit or two, but of late the symptoms are terrible. The phrenzy of the "Poems" was bad enough in its way, but it did not alarm us half so seriously as the calm, settled, imperturbable driveling idiocy of *Endymion*. It is a better and a wiser thing to be a starved apothecary than a starved poet, so back to the [apothecary] shop, Mr. John, back to plasters, pills, and ointment boxes.[4]

What writer has ever suffered a more heinous attack? What critic has ever made such a total ass and complete fool of himself?

Later nineteenth-century readers responded differently, embracing Keats as a poet of beauty, one who not only wrote about beauty but also created it; in fact, in the words of the contemporary poet Andrew Motion, the Victorians found Keats's poetry to be "more heavily loaded with sensualities, more gorgeous in its effects, more voluptuously alive to actualities than any poet who had come before him."[5] Writing about

"The Eve of St. Agnes," one writer extolled its "gorgeous gallery of poetic pictures." The poet William Michael Rossetti believed the poem, however, to "mean next to nothing."[6]

The poet Keats and the man John Keats stand, and act, in a relationship perhaps best described as symbiotic. We can trace, thanks particularly to the Letters, an evolution from life to art, and in the verse in particular we find everywhere a compassionate display of a movement from art to life. Keats's was no selfish, or preening, commitment to poetry, or deaf claim to a high poetic destiny fostered in burnished dreams. Poetry was no aesthetic escape, the poet no fevered dreamer. Poetry Keats saw as a made-thing of great beauty, bearing consolation for men and women inevitably and ineluctably subject to "circumstances" often horrific and frequently deadly. Beauty and truth he understood as locked in an inseparable, "perplexed" but affirmative embrace, whose tenderness it was the poet's calling to repeat.

Still, images persist to this day of John Keats as like the "pale-mouthed prophet dreaming" that he himself associated with Jesus in "Ode to Psyche." But in fact, he was no "eunuch in passion" (as he said the character Porphyro is not in "The Eve of St. Agnes").[7] His poems are sensual, as well as sensuous, and he is neither lacking in ideas nor dreaming his life away. John Keats was, in fact, exactly what his letters show: a man of great strength, compassion, selflessness, and courage, as well as talent and genius. He appears as the virtual opposite of what he labels, in the letters, as "the wordsworthian or egotistical sublime": "Every man has his speculations, but every man does not brood and peacock over them till he makes a false coinage and deceives himself."[8] You feel, reading the letters and the poems, that Keats has earned the right to speak and that the consolations he finds are realistic and deserved.

The man and the poet meet in understanding born of loss, pain, and suffering, understanding fired in the crucible of experience, the satisfactions of which it is aware and teaching, the product not merely of survival but of the purification that the encounters with hell have rendered. The letters we find to be so warm and engaging, compassionate and caring, because of the character of the voice we hear in them, a voice that we readily believe to be the man's, the man incarnate in his words. The letters reflect constantly on the theme that Keats knew supremely well, first-hand, in fact, and intimately: that of mutability (the perennial Romantic theme, of course).

T.S. Eliot wrote of Keats only once, this in "Shelley and Keats," included in *The Use of Poetry and the Use of Criticism*, the Norton

Lectures given at Harvard University in 1933 and published the following year. The essay devotes the bulk of attention to Shelley, turning to Keats only in the last three pages. It is important, though, Eliot perspicacious, in accounting for the Letters and characterizing the man and the writer. Eliot does so precisely in the context of treating the poet (in general) as also a philosopher.

> Keats seems to me . . . a great poet. I am not happy about *Hyperion*: it contains great lines, but I do not know whether it is a great poem. The Odes—especially perhaps the *Ode to Psyche*—are enough for his reputation. But I am not so much concerned with the degree of his greatness as with its kind; and its kind is manifested more clearly in his Letters than in his poems; . . . it seems to me to be much more the kind of Shakespeare. The Letters are certainly the most notable and the most important ever written by any English poet.[9]

Having made that major point, Eliot moves immediately to confront the issue facing any person who writes in an autobiographical form:

> Keats's egotism, such as it is, is that of youth which time would have redeemed. His letters are what letters ought to be; the fine things come in unexpectedly, neither introduced nor shown out, but between trifle and trifle.[10]

Eliot adds that Keats's observations on Wordsworth, in an 1817 letter to Benjamin Bailey, from which he proceeds to quote, "are of the finest quality of criticism, and the deepest penetration"—high praise, indeed.[11]

Since I will not return to the specific passages that Eliot quotes, I will adduce them here—Keats is talking in the first about Wordsworth's "Gypsy":

> It seems to me that if Wordsworth had thought a little deeper at that moment, he would not have written the poem at all. I should judge it to have been written in one of the most comfortable moods of his life—it is a kind of sketchy intellectual landscape, not a search for truth.[12]

We see in these words an essential congruity between Eliot and Keats, which has to do with the positive power of *difficulty*. Further, Keats critically juxtaposes sketchiness with the deep thinking that he returns to in other asseverations against Wordsworth. Above all, Keats registers here the primacy for him of the "search for truth."

The second passage that Eliot quotes is from another letter a few days later to Keats's good friend Benjamin Bailey:

> In passing...I must say one thing that has pressed upon me lately, and increased my Humility and capability of submission—and that is this truth— Men of Genius are great as certain ethereal chemicals operating on the Mass of neutral intellect—but they have not any individuality, any determined character—I would call the top and head of those who have a proper self Men of Power.[13]

Eliot singles out for mention and praise Keats's humility, willingness to submit, and skepticism regarding individuality (in this connection, Eliot might have noted the letter of 27 October 1818 to Richard Woodhouse, in which Keats animadverts against "the wordsworthian or egotistical sublime" and claims, in remarks anticipating Eliot's own regarding the poet's lack of personality, that the "poetical character" "has no self").[14]

Speaking of Keats's remarks in the second quoted passage, Eliot adds that such, "when made by a man so young as was Keats, can only be called the result of genius." Eliot proceeds:

> There is hardly one statement of Keats about poetry, which, when considered carefully and with due allowance for the difficulties of communication, will not be found to be true; and what is more, true for greater and more mature poetry than anything that Keats ever wrote.[15]

From these laudatory remarks, Eliot moves to end the essay "Shelley and Keats" with these summary statements that also stand as contextualizing and insightful sentences. Among other things, you notice here the basis of Eliot's own commentary in comparison and contrast, which he called one of the two "tools" of criticism, the other being "analysis."[16]

> Keats's sayings about poetry, thrown out in the course of private correspondence, keep poetry close to intuition; and they have no apparent bearing upon his own times, as he himself does not appear to have taken any absorbing interest in public affairs—though when he did turn to such matters, he brought to bear a shrewd and penetrating intellect. Wordsworth had a very delicate sensibility to social life and social changes.

Wordsworth and Shelley both theorise. Keats has no theory, and to have formed one was irrelevant to his interests, and alien to his mind. If we take either Wordsworth or Shelley as representative of his age, as being a voice of the age, we cannot so take Keats. But we cannot accuse Keats of any withdrawal, or refusal; he was merely about his business. He had no theories, yet in the sense appropriate to the poet, in the same sense, though to a lesser degree than Shakespeare, he had a 'philosophic' mind. He was occupied only with the highest use of poetry; but that does not imply that poets of other types may not rightly and sometimes by obligation be concerned about the other uses.[17]

So much, then, for the word still bruited about that Keats was little interested in, or capable of, ideas.

Of all the letters, the long one to George and Georgiana, dated 14 February to 3 May 1819, is perhaps the most intriguing. Especially the section dated 21 April represents another, more ambitious (and more successful) attempt to explain human life in terms of developing understanding, which Keats first broached in a letter to John Hamilton Reynolds, on 3 May of the previous year. There, at some length, in his own words, he "put[s] down a simile of human life as far as I now perceive it; that is, to the point to which I say we both have arrived at." Keats then launches into this surmise: "I compare human life to a large Mansion of Many Apartments, two of which I can only describe, the doors of the rest being as yet shut upon me." The first of these is "the infant or thoughtless Chamber, in which we remain as long as we do not think" and "notwithstanding the doors of the second Chamber remain wide open, showing a bright appearance, we care not to hasten to it; but are at length imperceptibly impelled by the awakening of the thinking principle—within us." The second chamber Keats calls "the Chamber of Maiden-Thought," in which when "we become intoxicated with the light and the atmosphere, we see nothing but pleasant wonders, and think of delaying there for ever in delight."[18] Apparent once more is Keats's perhaps surprising interest in and commitment to "thinking," which he finds deficient in Wordsworth.

Whereas this first attempt at explaining how human understanding develops over time derives from a sense of organic growth and natural development, the later, more sophisticated proposal is based entirely on the wonder-working of suffering in the development of a *soul*. Still, in the letter from I have just been quoting, Keats returns to the inescapable fact of suffering in human life. The writing has grown deeper and richer:

> However among the effects this breathing is father of is that tremendous one of sharpening one's vision into the ~~head~~ heart and nature of Man—of convincing ones nerves that the World is full of Misery and Heart-break, Pain, Sickness and oppression—whereby this Chamber of Maiden Thought becomes gradually darken'd and at the same time on all sides of it many doors are set open—but all dark—all leading to dark passages—We see not the balance of good and evil. We are in a Mist—*We* are now in that state— We feel the "burden of the Mystery."[19] . . .

This was the point, Keats figures, at which Wordsworth had arrived in "Tintern Abbey." He proceeds to other literary speculations, soon expanding into surmises regarding culture and history. "What is then to be inferr'd?" he asks. "O many things—It proves there is really a grand march of intellect—, It proves that a mighty providence subdues the mightiest Minds to the service of the time being, whether it be in human Knowledge or Religion."[20] Clearly, such grand questions lay at the forefront of Keats's thinking, simmering; thus his attempt in the 21 April 1819 letter to account for this "vale of Soul-making" was for Keats much more than an ephemeral or passing interest or concern.

The letter includes a reiteration of the suffering nature of human living: in this world, "we cannot expect to give way many hours to pleasure." Keats then mentions one of his recurring notions: "Circumstances are like Clouds continually gathering and bursting—While we are laughing the seed of some trouble is put into ~~he~~ the wide arable land of events—while we are laughing it sprouts is [sic] grows and suddenly bears a poison fruit which we must pluck. . . . "[21] By the 21st of April, Keats has been reading, pondering, surmising further, and reaching some thoughtful conclusions: "I have been reading lately two very different books Robertson's America and Voltaire's Siecle De Louis XIV It is like walking arm and arm between Pizarro and the great-little Monarch."[22] The poet is led into reflections on "the Protection of Providence," thence to these thoughts, deriving from the fundamental fact of human suffering and confirming the idea of "circumstances" as key to his thinking: "The whole appears to resolve into this—that Man is originally 'a poor forked creature' subject to the same mischances as the beasts of the forest, destined to hardships and disquietude of some kind or other." With each stage of improvement of "his bodily accom[m]odations and comforts," he goes on, "there are waiting for him a fresh set of annoyances." At this point, Keats waxes more affirmative:

> [man] is mortal and there is still a heaven with its Stars abov[e] his head. The most interesting question that can come before us is, How far by the persevering endeavours of a seldom appearing Socrates Mankind may be made happy—I can imagine such happiness carried to an extreme—but what must it end in?—Death—and who could in such a case bear with death—the whole troubles of life which are now frittered away in a series of years, would the[n] be accumulated for the last days of a being who instead of hailing its approach, would leave this world as Eve left Paradise—But in truth I do not believe in this sort of perfectibility—the nature of the world will not admit of it—the inhabitants of the world will correspond to itself. . . .[23]

Keats's reasoning is impressive, as is his knowledge of the world and of the human heart. He subscribes, apparently, to no *a priori* notions.

At this point, Keats begins his approach to the central idea of this letter, which is effectively centered around the fact of mutability. "The point at which Man may arrive," he writes, "is as far as the paral[l]el state in inanimate nature and no further," which appears as a qualifier of the optimism we have just seen. With a keen sense of effective detail, Keats asks his brother and sister-in-law to suppose that a rose has "sensation": "it blooms on a beautiful morning it enjoys itself—but comes a cold wind, a hot sun—It can not escape it, it cannot destroy its annoyances—they are as native to the world as itself: no more can man be happy in spite, the world[l]y elements will prey upon his nature. . . ."[24] The allegory is effective because simple and the terms familiar. Keats clearly wants his readers to understand him.

The heart of the matter now emerges at the fore, replete with another dig at Christianity (which generally occurs alongside confirmation of a belief in God, Providence, perhaps immortality and even heaven). Characteristically, Keats not only offers an alternative, but he does so by adopting basic terms shared with Christianity, which he then turns in another, certainly secular direction. Here, he also turns "world" and "soul" from "Diverse, sheer opposite, antipodes" into a relation with Incarnational overtones and perhaps structure: that is, the way to soul-making lies in, through, and by means of that which is usually construed to be the binary opposite:

> The common cognomen of this world among the misguided and super-stitious is "a vale of tears" from which we are to be redeemed by a certain arbit[r]ary interposition of God and taken to Heaven—What a little circum-scribe[d] straightened notion! Call the world if you Please "The vale of Soul-making" Then you will find out the use of the world (I am speaking now in the highest terms for human nature admitting it to be immortal which I will here take for granted for the purpose of showing a thought which has struck me concerning it) I say "*Soul making*" as distinguished from an Intelligence—There may be intelligences or sparks of divinity in millions—But they are not Souls the till they acquire identities, till each one is personally itself. I[n]telligences are atoms of perception—they know and they see and they are pure, in short they are God.[25]

From this controversial statement, Keats hurries on, without, however, moving away from his ideas or backing down. Indeed, he proceeds to another bold and defiant assertion: "How then are Souls to be made? How then are these sparks which are God to have identity given them—so as ever to possess a bliss peculiar to each ones individual existence?" Keats's recourse is to the idea of a "medium of a world like this." Well aware of his audacity, and showing the strength of his conviction, he adds: "This point I sincerely wish to consider because I think it a grander scheme of salvation than the chrysteain religion—or rather it is a system of Spirit-creation."[26]

The next concern is how to explain such "creation" or "making," with, perhaps, a slight echo of the earlier notion of a "Mansion of Many Apartments." "Three grand materials," he writes, may be understood as "acting the one upon the other for a series of years." These "Materials are the *Intelligence*—the *human heart* (as distinguished from intelligence or Mind) and the *World* or *Elemental space* suited for the proper action of *Mind and Heart* on each other for the purpose of forming the *Soul or Intelligence destined to possess the sense of Identity.*"[27] With somewhat more modesty and perhaps a smattering of humility, Keats then writes: "I can scarcely express what I but dimly perceive—and yet I think I perceive it." He adds: "that you may judge the more clearly I will put it in the most homely form possible."[28] What follows, is Keats's intense proposal regarding "The vale of Soul-making," the world represented as a school in which "the child" learns to read. The account becomes an apologia for the world and its suffering, delivered in the voice—appropriately enough—of a schoolmaster:

> I will call the *world* a School instituted for the purpose of teaching little children to read—I will call the *human heart* the *horn Book* used in that School—and I will call the *Child able to read, the Soul* made from that *school* and its *hornbook*. Do you not see how necessary a World of Pains and troubles is to school an Intelligence and make it a soul? A Place where the heart must feel and suffer in a thousand diverse ways! Not merely is the Heart a Hornbook, It is the Minds Bible, it is the Minds experience, it is the teat from which the Mind or intelligence sucks its identity—As various as the Lives of Men are—so various become their souls, and thus does God make individual beings, Souls, Identical Souls of the sparks of his own essence...."[29]

The voice of the schoolmaster, fitting in this context, appears in the question. Keats then pauses, teacher-like, to repeat the high estimation in which he holds his own described "system" and to justify the time he is taking and the effort he is asking of the recipients of his letter:

> This appears to me a faint sketch of a system of Salvation which does not affront our reason and humanity—I am convinced that many difficulties which christians labour under would vanish before it—there is one wh[i]ch even now Strikes me—the Salvation of Children—In them the Spark or Intelligence returns to God without any identity—it having had no time to learn of, and be altered by, the heart—or seat of the Passions—It is pretty generally suspected that the chrysteain scheme has been copied from the ancient persian and *greek* Philosophers.[30]

Keats appears to get carried away with his speculations, moving from a suggestive allegorical representation to wide-ranging claims regarding the efficacy of his "scheme." He emphasizes not just its simplicity but also its concrete nature, which he then opposes to "abstraction." He goes on: "Seriously I think it probable that this System of Soulmaking—may have been the Parent of all the more palpable and personal Schemes of Redemption, among the Zoroastrians the Christians and the Hindoos." He concludes, "For as one part of the human species must have carved their Jupiter; so another part must have the palpable and named Mediator and saviour, their Christ their Oromanes and their Vishnu ...."[31] Not yet finished, and ever the schoolmaster here, Keats now offers a recapitulation and summary, before finishing with several of his new poems.

> If what I have said should not be plain enough, as I fear it may not be, I will but [sic] you in the place where I began in this series of thoughts—I mean, I began by seeing how man was formed by circumstances—and what are circumstances?—but touchstones of his heart—? And what are touchstones?—but proovings of his hearrt? And what are proovings of his heart but fortifiers or alterers of his nature? And what is his altered nature but his soul?—and what was his soul before it came into the world and had These provings and alterations and perfectionings?—An intelligences—without Identity—and how is this Identity to be made through the Medium of the Heart? And how is the heart to become this Medium but in a world of Circumstances?[32]

Thus concludes the schoolmaster with his not-so-modest proposal.

That proposal we might—I believe it has never been done before—compare with Eliot's poem on the movement of "the simple soul" through life; I mean the third of his Ariel or Christmas poems *Animula*. *Animula*—the word means "soul"—begins with "the simple soul," said to "Issue . . . from the hand of God," through a second stage, focused as "The heavy burden of the growing soul," finally to a return to "the simple soul," said to "Issue . . . from the hand of time."[33] Eliot's poem, unlike Keats's ideas on "soul-making," is really concerned with much more than the effects of "circumstances" as such on the development of the soul.

Eliot's poem thus traces the soul's history, with its changes in character wrought by experience. As "issued," the soul finds itself in "a flat world," characterized by movement and change and taking pleasure in everyday, mundane things. In this first stage, the young soul "confounds the actual and the fanciful/Content with playing-cards and kings and queens,/What the faeries do and what the servants say." Things change as the soul "grows." With every passing day, it "Perplexes and offends more," "offends and perplexes more," as it is beset by "the imperatives of 'is and seems'/And may and may not, desire and control." This depiction recalls, in certain ways, the situation of "Lamia" and the account of the "unweaving" of the rainbow, which I have quoted as an epigraph above. Time, with the "circumstances" it brings, turns the "simple soul" into something "Irresolute and selfish,/misshapen, lame,/Unable to fare forward or retreat." Indeed, in a representation more Wordsworthian than Keatsian, Eliot paints the soul, rather Prufrock-like, as now "Fearing the warm reality, the offered good,/ Denying the importunity of the blood,/Shadow of its own shadows, spectre in its own gloom."

In *Animula*, no sign appears that time brings about the making of a soul. For Eliot, contrariwise, the soul exists from the beginning—although "Living first in the silence after the viaticum." In Eliot's poem, life, depicted as "the warm reality" (thus absent such "circumstances" as Keats knew all too well), reduces the soul, shrinks it, makes it both "irresolute" and "selfish," immobilizes it, in fact, thus rendering it ineffectual. Life—or "the world"—does not turn what Keats calls an "identity" into a soul; it is, rather, *there* at birth (becoming a spirit only after the viaticum has been pronounced), and what it encounters as the years pass— in other words, experience—is no teacher or text that affirms (positive) development. Keats is much more hopeful than Eliot—Eliot's Incarnational Christianity will not allow him to separate hope from its apparent opposite.

The letter in which occurs discussion of "The vale of Soul-making" is, in any case, not unproblematical. It is rife with imaginings and suppositions and comparisons. It reads, indeed, like an essay, with the writer trying on and out certain ideas and possibilities, weighing them, and then moving on. There is also the characteristic essayistic modesty and humility: "I can scarcely express what I but dimly perceive—and yet I think I perceive it." It is almost a dream. Then Keats follows with a felt necessity to express this dimly perceived matter "in the most homely form possible." It is clearly a trial.

I wonder if it may not also be more. The idea of "The vale of Soul-making" follows immediately upon an account of Keats's recent reading and sober reflections. I have quoted much of this earlier. It is certainly not a happy picture. Perhaps in face of these "circumstances" and limited, constrained happiness, Keats offers "The vale of Soul-making" as a thing of truth to his brother and sister-in-law that is represented precisely as a consolation, and nothing more nor less. That is, Keats begins, as he goes on in the letter to acknowledge, by seeing "how man was formed by circumstances," such experiences, in other words, that he knew all too well. He will then *turn* them, make positive, responsive use of them. That it is an essay—rather than a point of view to which he commits himself—is attested by the tumble of questions that he then raises, ending with this one: "And how is the heart to become this Medium but in a world of Circumstances?" Unlike in Eliot's *Animula*, the focus is squarely on the nature of reality (whereas Eliot's is on the soul). The possibilities Keats opens up in treating soul-making are, then, consolations, proposals, questions with possible answers—trials, *essays*. Since Keats does not pursue them in later letters or poems, I will conclude that, as consolations, they stand as possible temporary relief and a possibility only. I think the tentativeness of the whole effort here points to the fact that he felt comfortable that his letter's recipients would take his "grander system of salvation than the chrysteain religion" as he intended: a trial. It is one response to the nature of things; the idea of soul-making does not reappear to any significant degree in the poems, but other kinds of response do.

Whether my various surmises be valid, there can be little doubt that in the Letters Keats is thinking in, through, and by means of the writing; his reading and his reflections upon it have led to further thoughts, which he now expresses: there is little or no substantive editing or revising. What Keats writes down is what you get. And that present-ness, shall we call it, is one of the qualities that makes them valuable, providing an opportunity to look *through* them to large questions that they at least imply, consciously or not.

Reading the Letters in relation to Eliot's poem *Animula* allows us, as we have seen, to consider them as essays (just as *Animula* is an essay in poetic form, the Letters are essays as familiar correspondence). Differences are here at least as important as similarities: Keats reflects to a much greater than Eliot does, and the Letters represent the tentative character of essaying much more than does Eliot's poem. Reading what does not claim to be literature alongside a poem, which obviously does exist as literature, provides an opportunity—indeed, the impetus—to explore differences, in an effort, however Promethean, to apprehend just what it is that distinguishes literary writing, writing that can justly be called literature, from writing that makes no pretense to being more than it literally is. I too thus engage in essaying.

As exemplified in the way I have presented Keats's Letters, the term "literary," which does apply to at least some of this correspondence despite its occasional nature, refers to *what words do* and not just *what they say*. Non-literature is, contrariwise, writing concerned with meaning alone, with what words say, rather than how they work together—each word and phrase *supporting* "the others," as Eliot puts it. In this way, literature is indirect, whereas newspaper reporting, for example, is direct, concerned with what words say.[34] This means, furthermore, that literature is a thing Aristotelian rather than Platonic; what matters being internal, literature is, then, a thing of immanence.

But—and this is a huge caveat—literature precisely does not exist as a thing just immanent; it is also transcendent. Consider: in *Ash-Wednesday: Six Poems* and *Four Quartets*, his great long poems written after his formal conversion to Anglo-Catholic Christianity in 1927, Eliot both argues and dramatizes—thus combining essay and poetry, saying and doing—that the Word exists and functions "within/The world and for the world."[35] The Logos became embodied, that is to say, in the Incarnation of God in human form in the person of Jesus Christ. This transcendent power would thus, to follow the argument to its apparently logical conclusion, be present, even if and although "silent," by means of the very structure whereby "doing/working" appears alongside and within "saying."

Literature is, furthermore, like Christianity in being a thing of *rhyming*. By that word, I mean more than the technical, micro-matter whereby in the lines of verse end-words form parallel sounds with one another. I mean, instead, the macro-matter of analogical relations, whereby words, phrases, ideas, times, places, and scenes, for example, call to consciousness others, sometimes similar, sometimes different. Eliot calls it "supporting": "where every word is at home,/Taking its place to support the others." There is a whole, then, whose purpose we cannot know until we have reached the end, a whole made of (supporting) parts, whose significance we grasp, if at all, only when we have reached the end (where "the purpose breaks").

Although he was obviously no fan of Christianity, Keats had what I can only call a *religious instinct*. While ridiculing "the pious frauds of Religion," he honored Christ, whom he regarded as a "great" *man*, as one of only two people who "have had hearts comp[l[etely disinterested" (the other, he said, was Socrates).[36] As a token of Keats's position via-a-vis established religion, take the little-known, very frank sonnet "Written in Disgust of Vulgar Superstition," evidently composed during Christmas week 1816. Not published until 1876 (and not included in Douglas Bush's popular Riverside Edition of *Selected Poems and Letters*), this sonnet is a scathing attack, perhaps occasioned by the Holy Season and including bitter and angry dismissal of key movements in Christian liturgy and doctrine:

> The church bells toll a melancholy round,
>   Calling the people to some other prayers,
> Some other gloominess, more dreadful cares,
>   More heark'ning to the sermon's horrid sound.
>   Surely the mind of man is closely bound

> In some black spell; seeing that each one tears
> Himself from fireside joys, and Lydian airs,
> And converse high of those with glory crown'd.
> Still, still they toll, and I should feel a damp,
> A chill as from a tomb, did I not know
> That they are dying like an outburnt lamp;
> That 'tis their sighing, wailing ere they go
> Into oblivion;—that fresh flowers will grow,
> And many glories of immortal stamp.[37]

Christianity is thus depicted as anti-worldly, a transcendent thing that rips one apart from immanent pleasures; Keats associates it here and elsewhere with death.

Another of Keats's familiar ideas shows signs of rhyming with the "vale of Soul-making." I mean the famous "negative capability," discussed in a letter of late December 1817 to his brothers George and Thomas. First, Keats briefly points to how his mind was then working: "several things dovetailed in my mind, & at once it struck me, what quality went to form a Man of Achievement especially in Literature & which Shakespeare posessed so enormously." This he labels "*Negative Capability*," which he then proceeds to define in a manner that seems to belie his term:

> that is when man is capable of being in uncertainties, Mysteries, doubts, without any irritable reaching after fact & reason—Coleridge, for instance, would let go by a fine isolated verisimilitude caught from the Penetralium of mystery, from being incapable of remaining content with half knowledge. This pursued through Volumes would perhaps take us no further than this, that with a great poet the sense of Beauty overcomes every other considera- tion, or rather obliterates all consideration.[38]

Keats's idea reminds me of the Platonic *Metaxy*, that state consisting of tension and acceptance that also calls to mind T.S. Eliot on wit and both F. Scott Fitzgerald and James Baldwin on the ability to abide and embrace two conflicting ideas at once.[39] It is, finally, I suspect, related to Keats's fervent opposition to the Wordsworthian or "egotistical sublime," which he describes in a letter of 27 October 1818 to Richard Woodhouse, in terms highly suggestive of embracing paradox:

> As to the poetical Character itself, (I mean that sort of which, if I am any thing, I am a Member; that sort distinguished from the wordsworthian or

egotistical sublime; which is a thing per se and stands alone) it is not itself—
it has no self—it is every thing and nothing—It has no character—it enjoys
light and shade; it lives in gusto, be it foul or fair, high or low, rich or poor,
mean or elevated—It has as much delight in conceiving an Iago as an
Imogen. What shocks the virtuous philosop[h]er, delights the camelion
Poet. It does no harm from its relish of the dark side of things any more
than from its taste for the bright one; because they both end in speculation.
A Poet is the most unpoetical of any thing in existence; because he has no
Identity—he is continually in for—and filling some other Body—The Sun,
the Moon, the Sea and Men and Women who are creatures of impulse are
poetical and have about them an unchangeable attribute—the poet has
none; no identity—he is certainly the most unpoetical of all God's
Creatures.[40]

I find this confusing, for Keats begins by declaring himself a member of a
group of poets having a "poetical Character," which he fervently distinguishes from the "wordsworthian or egotistical sublime," who is, in turn,
a sort of poet with a definite and assertive identity. *That*, such a poet goes
about imposing, willfully. Almost immediately, though, "poetical" ceases
to be a neutral term and becomes an opprobrium; it, in fact, takes on the
very nature of the negative side of the previous opposition. Of course, the
terms are not what really matters here, which is the attempt to define the
poet, not only as different from the sublimely egotistical Wordsworth, but
as marked by such lack of willfulness, and indeed "personality," as T.S.
Eliot honored in defining the poet—also opposite Wordsworth—as lacking in personality ("Tradition and the Individual Talent").

We come back, at the end of this chapter on Keats's letters, directly to
who he understands the poet to be and what he considers the poetic
responsibility to be. It is not the voice of the schoolmaster that we hear
elsewhere in the letters and certainly not in the poems. Perhaps no better
figure exists for describing the man and the poet than what Keats provides
in *The Fall of Hyperion: A Dream*, verses that pick up a number of vital
themes:

> ... sure a poet is a sage;
> A humanist, physician to all men. (1.189–90)

Indeed, in the figure of the physician, Keats the man and Keats the poet
come together. In the same passage, Keats proceeds to describe the poet

more particularly, the terms directly recalling those used in "Sleep and Poetry," written in the last months of 1816:

> the great end
> Of poesy, that it should be a friend
> To sooth the cares, and lift the thoughts of man. (245–47)

Then, in *The Fall of Hyperion: A Dream*, a continuation of the ideas just quoted from that poem:

> The poet and the dreamer are distinct,
> Diverse, sheer opposite, antipodes.
> The one pours out a balm upon the world,
> The other vexes it. (1.199–202)

"Sleep and Poetry" proceeds to the following elaboration, putting in other words what the later poem will develop—and what Keats always made the end and the result of his poetic practice:

> As she was wont, th' imagination
> Into most lovely labyrinths will be gone,
> And they shall be accounted poet kings
> Who simply tell the most heart-easing things. (255–58)

The venue for, and the means of, conveying that "balm," we will see, is beauty. In a letter written to his friend Benjamin Bailey on the 22nd of November 1817, Keats broached the idea of beauty and its relation to truth:

> I am certain of nothing but of the holiness of the Heart's affections and the truth of imagination—What the Imagination seizes as Beauty must be truth—whether it existed before or not—for I have the same idea of all our Passions as of Love they are All in their sublime, creative of essential Beauty.... [41]

And of course, the "Ode on a Grecian Urn" famously ends with enigmatically punctuated verses, about which scholars have spilled so much ink over the years:

> Beauty is truth, truth Beauty,—that is all
> Ye know on earth, and all ye need to know.

"[T]he excellence of every Art," he wrote in a letter of late December 1817 to George and Georgiana, "is its intensity, capable of making all disagreeables evaporate, from their being in close relationship with Beauty."[42]

There is also the extended discussion in the "Epistle to John Hamilton Reynolds," written in late March 1818, which sounds remarkably prescient:

> O that our dreamings all, of sleep or wake,
> Would all their colours from the sunset take:
> From something of material sublime,
> Rather than shadow our own soul's day-time
> In the dark void of night. For in the world
> We jostle,—but my flag is not unfurl'd
> On the admiral-staff,—and to philosophise
> I dare not yet! Oh, never will the prize,
> High reason, and the lore of good and ill,
> Be my award! Things cannot to the will
> Be settled, but they tease us out of thought;
> Or is it that imagination brought
> Beyond its proper bound, yet still confin'd,
> Lost in a sort of Purgatory blind,
> Cannot refer to any standard law
> Of either earth or heaven? It is a flaw
> In happiness, to see beyond our bourn,—
> It forces us in summer skies to mourn,
> It spoils the singing of the nightingale. (67–85)

"Material sublime" perhaps says it all (even if we do not contrast it with the "wordsworthian or egotistical sublime"). Keats often appears very much an immanentist. He may never "philosophise"—if we mean by "philosophy" the thinking that, according to the later "Lamia," "unweaves" a rainbow—though he certainly does engage, even centrally, with ideas. Indeed, in ways general and specific, the "Epistle to John Hamilton Reynolds" anticipates "Lamia," its point of view quite similar.

Certainly, as Victorians appreciated, Keats's own poetry is rife with beautiful tableaux, fulfilling the declaration with which he opens *Endymion*, a sustained statement of powerful feeling and equally powerful belief and faith:

> A thing of beauty is a joy for ever:
> Its loveliness increases; it will never

> Pass into nothingness; but still will keep
> A bower quiet for us, and a sleep
> Full of sweet dreams, and health, and quiet breathing.
> Therefore, on every morrow, are we wreathing
> A flowery band to bind us to the earth,
> Spite of despondence, of the inhuman dearth
> Of noble natures, of the gloomy days,
> Of all the unhealthy and o'er-darkened ways
> Made for our searching: yes, in spite of all,
> Some shape of beauty moves away the pall
> From our dark spirits. (1.1–13)

Whatever he may mean elsewhere regarding the relation of beauty and truth, here he refuses to separate beauty and the truth of the human condition.

In "The Eve of St. Agnes," full of beautiful tableaux, beauty exists in and as both the sensuous and the sensual, delivered in rich and luxurious Spenserian stanzas, about which more in a later chapter. After the luxuriously described feast of the senses in that poem, the passion, the beauty, and the love, conveyed in language and verse the perfect corollary, Keats—the truth-teller as well as the poet of beauty—ends "The Eve of St. Agnes" by making sure that his reader is under no illusions about what is possible in this world (of "circumstances")—the lovers Madeline and Porphyro flee, but into the raging storm, while the symbol of Christian asceticism merely dies, *unclaimed* by the God to Whom he sacrificed himself. Beauty—in all its manifestations—may be the only satisfactory, effectual response to mutability and suffering.

The little-known sonnet "The Grasshopper and the Cricket," written on 30 December 1816, focuses on the theme in *Endymion* regarding the salutary, if not salvific, ministrations of the earth and its beauties and delights, further "soothing" us and "lifting our thoughts"—a minor and early sort of anticipation of "To Autumn" in theme and a special linking of earthly delights as "poesy":

> The poetry of earth is never dead:
>   When all the birds are faint with the hot sun,
>   And hide in cooling trees, a voice will run
> From hedge to hedge about the new-mown mead;
> That is the Grasshopper's—he takes the lead
>   In summer luxury,—he has never done

> With his delights; for when tired out with fun
> He rests at ease beneath some pleasant weed.
> The poetry of earth is ceasing never:
>   On a lone winter's evening, when the frost
> Has wrought a silence, from the stove there shrills
> The Cricket's song, in warmth increasing ever,
>   And seems to one in drowsiness half lost,
> The Grasshopper's among some grassy hills.

I will conclude this chapter with specific reference to the little-known but wonderful "Fragment of an Ode to Maia," written on May-Day 1818 and copied into a letter of 3 May to John Hamilton Reynolds. Douglas Bush has said this of the poem, a statement that alone justifies our pausing briefly to consider it:

> This fragment—which needs nothing more—is one of Keats's most serene and felicitous affirmations on the side of passive, non-intellectual receptivity to concrete impressions.[43]

The poem, I think, helps to summarize the arguments of this chapter, thence to point the way to the next chapter, on the poems. Here is the "Fragment of an Ode to Maia":

> Mother of Hermes! And still youthful Maia!
>   May I sing to thee
> As thou wast hymned on the shores of Baiae?
>   Or may I woo thee
> In earlier Sicilian? Or thy smiles
> Seek as they once were sought, in Grecian isles,
> By bards who died content on pleasant sward,
>   Leaving great verse unto a little clan?
> O, give me their old vigour, and unheard
>   Save of the quiet primrose, and the span
>   Of heaven and few ears,
> Rounded by thee, my song should die away
>   Content as theirs,
> Rich in the simple worship of a day.

Maia is a complex mythological figure, with meaning and significance in both Greek and Roman mythology. Zeus, it is said, fathered Hermes upon Maia,

who shied away from the company of the Gods. It has also been said that the
month of May is named for Maia. Keats's little poem, which happens to have
(the sonnet form's) 14 lines and to exhibit a clear difference between the
eighth and ninth verses, is both playful and respectful: note the play, for
instance, on the adjoining words "Maia" and "May" (the verb) in the opening
two verses. And more: The last verse at once places matters in a context
brimful of religious instinct and asserts the immanence, presence, and imme-
diacy of responsible "worship": that of "a day." It may not, then, be quite
enough to describe the poem as an affirmation of "passive, non-intellectual
receptivity to concrete impressions." The intellect *is* involved, the poem is, in
fact, affirmative, and Keats stresses receptivity, but he does so in a framework
of attentive myth, the capaciousness of allusion, evident philosophic concern,
and a strong and abiding sense of responsibility to and for suffering
humanity.[44]

NOTES

1. The standard biography is by Walter Jackson Bate, *John Keats* (Cambridge, MA: Belknap-Harvard UP, 1979).
2. For such publication history, see, for example, Bate.
3. *The Quarterly Review*, April 1818, 204–8 (quoted in wikipedia)
4. *Blackwood's Edinburgh Magazine,* 3 (1818), 519–24 (*Nineteenth Century Literary Manuscripts*), quoted in wikipedia.
5. Andrew Motion, *The Guardian,* 23 January 2010, quoted in wikipedia.
6. Hugh Miller, *Essays* (London, 1856–62), 1.452; and William Michael Rossetti, *Life of John Keats* (London, 1887), 183.
7. John Keats, *The Letters of John Keats*, ed. Hyder E. Rollins (Cambridge, MA: Harvard UP, 1958), 2:163.
8. See Grant Scott, "Keats in His Letters," in *Poetry and Prose of John Keats.* Norton Critical Editions. (New York: Norton, 2008): 555–63.
9. T.S. Eliot, *The Use of Poetry and the Use of Criticism: Studies in the Relation of Criticism to Poetry in England* (London: Faber and Faber, 1933), 100.
10. Ibid.
11. Ibid.
12. Quoted, Ibid., 100–1.
13. Ibid., 101.
14. Keats, *Selected Poems and Letters*, 279.
15. Eliot, *The Use of Poetry and the Use of Criticism*, 101.

16. Eliot, *The Sacred Wood: Essays on Poetry and Criticism* (London: Methuen, 1920), 33.
17. Eliot, *The Use of Poetry and the Use of Criticism*, 102.
18. Keats, *Selected Poems and Letters*, 274.
19. Ibid.
20. Ibid., 275.
21. Ibid., 284.
22. Ibid., 287.
23. Ibid., 287–88.
24. Ibid., 288.
25. Ibid.
26. Ibid.
27. Ibid.
28. Ibid., 288–89.
29. Ibid., 289.
30. Ibid.
31. Ibid.
32. Ibid.
33. T.S. Eliot, *Animula* (London: Faber and Faber, 1929). On Keats's letters, see Grant Scott, *"Keats in His Letters,"* in the *Norton Critical Edition of Keats's Poetry and Prose*, ed. Jeffrey N. Cox (New York: Norton, 2008), 555–63; and Susan J. Wolfson, *Reading John Keats* (Cambridge: Cambridge UP, 2015), passim.
34. T.S. Eliot, *Four Quartets* (New York: Harcourt, Brace, 1943).
35. T.S. Eliot, *Ash-Wednesday: Six Poems* (London: Faber and Faber, 1930).
36. Ibid., 285.
37. In *The Poems of John Keats*, ed. Jack Stillinger (Cambridge, MA: Belknap-Harvard UP, 1978), 88.
38. Keats, *Selected Poems and Letters*, 261.
39. See T.S. Eliot, "Andrew Marvell," *Selected Essays*, 3rd ed. (London: Faber and Faber, 1951), 303; F. Scott Fitzgerald, "The Crack-Up," *The Crack-Up*, ed. Edmund Wilson (New York: New Directions, 1945), 69; James Baldwin, "Notes of a Native Son," *Notes of a Native Son* (Boston, MA.: Beacon Press, 1955), 113.
40. Keats, *Selected Poems and Letters*, 279.
41. Ibid., 257–58.
42. Ibid., 260.
43. Ibid., 330.
44. The best discussion of Keats and religion remains, in my judgment, Ronald A. Sharp, *Keats, Skepticism, and the Religion of Beauty* (Athens: U of Georgia P, 1979). It is perhaps not surprising that at points our treatments take parallel lines, both of us having been students of E.D. Hirsch at the

University of Virginia, he in the 70s, me in the 60s. My original article on "The Eve of St. Agnes" preceded Sharp's book by some 6 years. Sharp essentially defines Keats's religious position by means of the supposed compatibility of its skepticism and aestheticism. In the end, Sharp finds in Keats a "new and radically untraditional humanized religion," a religion of beauty (4). Although I remain interested in Keats's "religious instinct" (as I prefer to call it), I am more concerned here with prior matters, especially how we read the poetry, what Keats's words say, and how the poems actually work.

CHAPTER 3

Some of the Dangers in "Unperplex[ing] bliss from its neighbour pain": Reading the Odes Intra- and Inter-textually

Abstract The six great Odes are considered separately as well as in thematic order, beginning with "Indolence" and ending with the magisterial "To Autumn." Enabling a fresh reading of the poems is a close comparison of each with apposite passages in T.S. Eliot's poems; the result of this comparative venture is a fresh sense of Keats's interest in and treatment of ideas, once thought to be lacking in his poems. Considered together, the Odes explore ideas of beauty and truth and their necessary relation. Keats is seen as working toward greater and greater "impersonality," "To Autumn" standing as a significant poetic achievement.

Keyword Thematic order of Odes · Comparison with Eliot · Ideas · Impersonality · "To Autumn"

> So threw the goddess off, and won his heart
> More pleasantly by playing woman's part,
> With no more awe than what her beauty gave,
> That, while it smote, still guaranteed to save.
>
> —"Lamia"

> Ay, in the very temple of Delight
>   Veil'd Melancholy has her Sovran shrine....
>
> —"Ode on Melancholy"

© The Author(s) 2016
G.D. Atkins, *On Keats's Practice and Poetics of Responsibility*,
DOI 10.1007/978-3-319-44144-3_3

So it is, Keats would tell us, when the poet comes to realise that his longing aspirations after beauty and perfection in his poetry, and his passionate desire to serve his fellow creatures, are not conflicting ideals, but are one and the same; that for him to use faithfully and earnestly his poetic gift is to render the highest service to mankind, that he has become a true poet.

Henry Clement Nottcut, *An Interpretation of Keats's "Endymion"*

Reading Keats's poems requires a very different set of skills and expectations from those entailed in reading T.S. Eliot's, as I have been doing for many years now. Especially in the verses written after his 1927 formal embrace of Anglo-Catholic Christianity via baptism into the Church of England, Eliot followed the example and the "theory" of seventeenth-century Bishop Lancelot Andrewes and "squeezed" words for their "full juice of meaning." That is to say, Eliot's reader must follow the Modernist poet's own way of writing, and attend scrupulously to the meaning of every word and to the word's relation, in "its nearer and in its most remote contexts," in other words, a practice of comparative reading.[1]

In Keats's odes, "squeezing" of individual words yields relatively little. Emphasis lies elsewhere: for instance, on the pictures the words together "make" and the intensity of feeling that the poet expresses through especially loaded words and phrases. Keats seems to me most interesting, and effective, when he tells a story, rather than "states," even if there is, as in "Ode on Melancholy," a decided movement of represented ideas. Narrative leads to both intra- and inter-textuality, involving comparative reading (after all), of the sort that impels the reader forward and backward and compels her or his attention. Appreciation, enjoyment, and understanding of the individual Odes is considerably enriched by reading them together, comparing and contrasting their themes, strategies, voice, and point of view.

In this regard, I join ranks with Helen Vendler's monumental study *The Odes of John Keats* (1985). Widely considered to be the pre-eminent American close-reader of poetry, Vendler provides superb historical and contextual background, from which her readings spring—and yet, I turn from her pages with an unsullied desire to see—with G. Wilson Knight—"from *within*" the verse. In my view, in both Vendler and Earl Wasserman, as valuable as their books undeniably are, the erudition is so heavy, and they are so dependent on it, that a shadow falls between their reading and the text, sometimes aborting our effort to understand it. The commentator's own abundantly capacious vision obscures the poems. Vendler's book on the six Odes plus *The Fall of Hyperion* runs to 330 packed pages.

In part so as to offset the temptation to impose my own vision—and thus invite comparison with such as Vendler's and Wasserman's, Stuart Sperry's, and Susan Wolfson's—I am going to consider the Odes by comparing their subjects with Eliot's treatment of the same. The end is not some invidious comparison of either person or poet or poem, no ranking of insight or acquisition and expression of truth. The pre-eminent mode of commentary for Eliot, indeed one of the two tools of criticism, he said, comparison can enable recognitions and revelations unavailable when a text is considered by itself; it carries, in other words, inter- and intra-textual analysis one step further. The often quite different understanding found in Eliot's poetic art, when the two are compared, brings out aspects and ramifications of Keats's Odes that are, otherwise, liable to be missed.

The language of Keats's poems is highly artificial, and the stanzaic form is generally Elizabethan—this, until "Lamia" and "To Autumn," at least, at the very end. Character as such, in the Odes, and even in "The Eve of St. Agnes," matters little. There is next to nothing naturalistic in these poems, which is not a negative evaluation, but rather a description and a compara-tive judgment. Notwithstanding Keats's insistence on tying us to the earth, the poems exist as things apart, a separate creation from the "circumstances" that buffet, constrain, and destroy life. Accordingly, the personages in the poems are fictive, unmistakably so; they are occasions, devices, and means, not real people—thus so many bear "foreign" and mythological names. Keats tries hard to keep the representations in the poems separate from the world that his reader inhabits—in hopes of preventing such attempted carry-over, transfiguring and "translating," as dooms Lycius and Lamia.

The Odes—sometimes called "the great Odes"—consist, in apparent order of composition, of "Ode to Psyche," "Ode to Nightingale," "Ode on a Grecian Urn," "Ode on Melancholy," "Ode on Indolence," and "To Autumn," the first written in April 1819, the next four—incredibly—the following month, and "To Autumn" in September of the same year.[2] They were all published together in the magisterial third volume of Keats's verse: *Lamia, Isabella, The Eve of St. Agnes, and Other Poems*, in early July 1820.

Essentially written together, then (perhaps with the exception of "To Autumn," three to four months following the others), the Odes should, I think, be read together, as parts of a certain whole. I mean, they matter each in and of itself, but taken together, the six represent something other and more than the sum of the parts. Here, I propose, order does matter, but it is not, I further suggest, principally or necessarily chronological, the time difference involved in their composition being, after all, minimal. It is, rather, the order in which they are read that matters most, and that order depends upon the reader's discovery of critical elements, themes, and points of view deliverable by comparative, intra- and inter-textual considerations.

At least, Keats did not title his poem "Ode *to* Indolence." Still, though it is not one of his best odes, it has its virtues, among them an acute self-consciousness. Thus, in the sixth and final stanza, Keats bids adieu to the three ghostly figures that have thrice passed by his morning vision, seeking to rouse him from indolence (and indulgence). He identifies them as Love, Ambition, and his "demon Poesy." Temptation to escape pain, and the mentioned "nothingness," thus sidles alongside renewed recognition of mutability, and the desire for escape from pain that attends the original meaning of the word in Latin; in the end, Keats is, ironically, steadfast in clinging to indolent ways. There is much to admire here, and respect, whether or not including the potential self-accusation in the fourth verse down:

> So, ye three Ghosts, adieu! Ye cannot raise
>   My head cool-bedded in the flowery grass;
> For I would not be dieted with praise,
>   A pet-lamb in a sentimental farce!
> Fade softly from my eyes, and be once more
>   In masque-like figures on the dreamy urn;
>   Farewell! I yet have visions for the night,
> And for the day faint visions there is store;
>   Vanish, ye Phantoms! From my idol spright,
>   Into the clouds, and never more return!

Bringing Eliot to bear on the poem may seem supererogatory, if not perverse. But in fact the issue of indolence is not so far from Eliot's poetry as we might initially suppose (and by this I mean much more than the fact that in "East Coker" Eliot uses the far less familiar synonym "hebetude," meaning lethargy and dullness). Eliot is little interested in questions of ambition, it is true, nor, really, with romantic love. Nor does he, with Keats however melodramatical he is being, identify "Poesy" as a "demon." He does, however, often treat the vocation of poetry, in particular the difficulty it entails. Keats laments that "Poesy" pales in consolatory power beside indolence; consolation is needed precisely because of "change": "Poesy"

> has not a joy,—
> At least for me,—so sweet as drowsy noons,
> And evenings steep'd in honied indolence;
> O, for an age so shelter'd from annoy,
> That I may never know how change the moons,
> Or hear the voice of busy common-sense!

For Eliot, the problem—and he affirms that large difficulties attach to the making of poetry—lies in language and that resistance that comes between conception and expression, understanding and being understood. While agreeing in disliking change, Eliot does not lay all, or even most, blame at its door. He has "largely wasted" 20 years, he writes in "East Coker," "Trying to learn to use words"—because they refuse to "stay still." The movement of his verse being the movement of his thought, Eliot writes that

> every attempt
> Is a wholly new start, and a different kind of failure
> Because one has only learnt to get the better of words
> For the thing one no longer has to say, or the way in which
> One is no longer disposed to say it.[3]

The poet must, then, start over each time he turns to writing, and Eliot adds:

> there is no competition—
> There is only the fight to recover what has been lost
> And found and lost again and again: and now, under
> conditions
> That seem unpropitious. But perhaps neither gain nor loss.
> For us, there is only the trying. The rest is not our business.

In the context of Keats's poem, I cannot but hear a pun in Eliot's word "rest."

Eliot is concerned to understand, change not the issue so much as time itself. In place of consolation, Eliot looks toward understanding, which involves honest, straightforward self-examination and self-criticism (productive of humility). Keats stresses the temptation, its nature and its power; Eliot is concerned, not with moral issues or failure of character, but with the problematic of writing itself, a modern concern.

However unlikely, "Indolence" calls to my mind "The Love Song of J. Alfred Prufrock." To be sure, the titular speaker is not indolent, but he embodies the very hesitation before, and fear of, "faring forward" that often motivates the indolent. Desire of stasis, not so different either from the denial and repudiation of spring and new birth, identifies the sad inhabitants of *The Waste Land*. The other side of that desire is anxiety regarding the tensional nature of existence, the condition that *Ash-Wednesday* calls "the time of tension between dying and birth."[4] Tension occurs in the "Ode," of course, but it has to do with the possibility of the speaker's submission to indolence. Change clearly saddens, if it does not actually debilitate, Keats, but in this Ode he shows no sign of recognizing that he inhabits that "middle state" that also describes the condition in which the poet, willy-nilly, finds himself ("East Coker"). The avoidance of tension, the desire of indolence, very nearly becomes in Keats the quest of an anodyne, certainly a temptation that fuels an ever-present drama. At the same time, he affirms at the end that he has enough "visions" in "store" for both night and day.

Such comparison as that in which we have just engaged, between Keats and Eliot, perhaps reaches its most telling point, at least insofar as "Ode on Indolence" is concerned, with the adduction from "East Coker" of the words "We must be still and still moving/Into another intensity." "Intensity" has the same root as "tension," but I will merely note it, for now focusing on "still and still moving," an "impossible union" and a "necessarye coniunction." These four simple words capture, exemplify, and incarnate the paradoxical understanding/the understanding of paradox that everywhere marks Eliot's understanding, at least post-conversion to Anglo-Catholic Christianity.

Whereas, then, Keats is tempted toward stillness—a recurring concern in his poems—Eliot refuses to separate stillness from its apparent opposite, accepting the tensional nature of our being and our world: "Fare forward," he insists. *Comparison* participates in the same essential structure, for in pinpointing, specifying, and distinguishing, it eschews the separation of one thing from another. Doubleness prevails here too, instead of a singular thing by itself.

"Ode to Psyche" is a better poem, though not one of Keats's very best Odes, in my judgment. "Indolence" is a state, an abstraction, Psyche of course a goddess. The poem is another manifestation of Keats's quest for a durable God, in a world in which the Christian Deity has not disappeared but appears ineffective and even irrelevant. In this Ode, Keats begins by addressing the "Goddess," the beautiful young girl of classical mythology, who was loved by Eros; she personifies the soul, in Neoplatonism, becoming an emanation of the One, seen as the world's animating principle and universal consciousness. Within days of writing "Ode to Psyche," Keats said in a letter dated 21 April 1819 that it was "the first and the only one with which I have taken even moderate pains—I have for the most part dash'd off[f] my lines in a hurry—This I have done leisurely." He added: "I think it reads the more richly for it." As to what he was doing in the poem, Keats offered, in the same letter to George and Georgiana, valuable commentary, in which he shows, not necessarily a schoolmaster's pedantry but the well-stocked mind of a poet distinct from a "versifying pet-lamb":

> You must recollect that Psyche was not embodied as a goddess before the time of Apulieus [sic] the Platonist who lived after the A[u]gustan age, and consequently the Goddess was never worshipped or sacrificed to with any of the ancient fervour—and perhaps never thought of in the old religion—I am more orthodox that [sic] to let a he[a]then Goddess be so neglected.[5]

In *The Golden Ass*, the second-century Latin writer Apuleius reads Psyche's story as an allegory of the Soul's progress guided by Love. It had to appeal to Keats, who, in the Ode, represents himself—or, rather, the speaker—as Psyche's priest.

Keats opens the poem by wondering if he had dreamt, or had seen the "wing'd Psyche with awaken'd eyes." He says he had "wander'd in a forest thoughtlessly," then saw "two fair creatures, couched side by side." He adds that "The winged boy I knew;/But who was thou, O happy, happy dove?/His Psyche true!" Keats then launches into a paean to Psyche that includes laments that, though she is "Fairer" than others in "Olympus' faded hierarchy," "temple thou hast none": no flower-draped altar, no "virgin-choir," nor voice, lute, pipe, no "incense sweet/From chain-swung censer teeming;/No shrine, no grove, no oracle, no heat/Of pale-mouth'd prophet dreaming." With these last words, Keats seems unable to refrain from a gratuitous remark regarding institutional Christianity as well as Jesus.

In the fourth stanza (of five), Keats contextualizes, as it were, his lament: Psyche was "too late for antique vows" and "for the fond believing lyre." Gone are the days "When holy were the haunted forest boughs,/Holy the air, the water, and the fire." Those days of pagan immanence are no more. As well, the days of the poet's life are "far retir'd/From happy pieties." Yet he is inspired by his "own eyes," and asks Psyche to allow him to "be thy choir, and make a moan/Upon the midnight hours." The last four verses of the stanza come very close to repeating word-for-word the last four of the preceding stanza, both directed against the (repeated) "pale-mouth'd prophet dreaming." For Keats, "dreaming" is a thing not to be indulged, but subjected to exposure.

Keats ends "Ode to Psyche" with a proclamation of commitment, pledging to build for the Goddess a "sanctuary" in his mind: "Yes, I will be thy priest, and build a fane/In some untrodden region of my mind," in the quietness of a "sanctuary" made of beauties nature affords, and "there shall be for thee all soft delight/That shadowy thought can win,/A bright torch, and a casement ope at night,/To let the warm Love in!" The connection with the desire, as well as the drive, evinced in the account of "the vale of Soul-making" is obvious. With the "Ode to Psyche," another voice is added to the array of voices that characterizes Keats's poetic embodiment: "priest" thus joins with "sage," "humanist, physician," and truth-teller and poet of beauty. It is important to note that, as Walter Jackson Bate demonstrated long ago, Keats's propensity for past participles, as above, reflects an understanding of the taut, kept force within even the inanimate.[6]

And about that voice: I have uneasily talked of both Keats and "the speaker." In truth, the poem is not a lyric—if by "lyric" we mean the expression of the poet's own feelings. Keats opposed such "preening" as he says Wordsworth does, talking at length about himself and even his meanest experiences, and so Keats's speakers in the Odes are neither historically nor biographically situated; nor are they individualized in any way. To a degree, the speaker is not different from the poet; rather, Keats actually seems to collapse or dissolve into a larger "I" who is (also) a poet. The voice we hear in the Odes is, in short, a universal poetic voice, not to be simply *identified* with Keats nor distanced from him either as involving different points of view and values.

And as to Psyche, which, like "animula," means "soul," the Ode's treatment differs radically from that in the letters, in which the soul is said to be made by "circumstances." Both Keatsian representations differ from Eliot's; in the Ariel or Christmas poem *Animula*, which I treat elsewhere in this book, the soul is said to come directly from God. It is certainly no god or goddess.

"Ode on Melancholy" is a short poem, consisting of 30 lines, divided into three equal stanzas. It is one of Keats's most powerful poems. "Melancholy" seems the exact term for capturing and tightly holding the effects of the world on the soul, "circumstances," and pervasive loss, pain, and suffering. The poem gives the lie, despite the temptations dramatized variously in the Odes, to the accusations that Keats was a dreamer who sought escape from this world, its mutability, and its horror. The poem also connects, directly and fundamentally, with the "Ode on Indolence," assuming the perspective of and representing the understanding of that absent from what is actually the later poem.

The point is established with, and acquires great power from, the emphatic first, certain words, addressed not to Melancholy, but instead to the reader or Keats's fellow-sufferer. The injunction is to bypass usual anodynes (with a pointed dismissal of a "rosary of yew-berries") and turn instead to embrace, ultimately, the very anguish driving you to seek relief and ultimately some sort of transcendence—it is implicit repudiation of the falsehood perpetrated in the "unreal" cities of *The Waste Land*.

> No, no, go not to Lethe, neither twist
>   Wolf's-bane, tight-rooted, for its poisonous wine;
> Nor suffer thy pale forehead to be kiss'd
>   By nightshade, ruby grape of Proserpine;
> Make not your rosary of yew-berries,
>   Nor let the beetle, nor the death-moth be
> Your mournful Psyche, nor the downy owl
> A partner in your sorrow's mysteries;
>   For shade to shade will come too drowsily,
> And drown the wakeful anguish of the soul.

None of the vehicles of forgetfulness or escape will do. The innocent-looking word "rosary" in the fifth verse down not only affirms the religious instinct alive and working in Keats's imagination, but it also suggests the necessity of attending to Melancholy as Keats interprets and represents it here (the yew, familiar to readers of T.S. Eliot, symbolizes both mortality and immortality).[7] Rather, then, than "drown" the soul's suffering, embrace, says the poem, the very "anguish" that, awake and percipient, it knows only too well.

Indeed, continues Keats in the second stanza, Melancholy will befall you, and when, willy-nilly, it does, the thing to do is simple, if not always obvious to us. The form of the poem is, thus, rational and logical: "Then glut thy sorrow on a morning rose,/Or on the rainbow of the salt sand-wave,/Or on the wealth of globed peonies." But if— now turning specific—"thy mistress some rich anger show,/Emprison her soft hand, and let her rave,/And feed deep, deep upon her peerless eyes." The verb "glut" captures the very earthiness that Keats has in mind along with the unstinting nature of the proposed "cure." The solution is not easy; it is precisely hard, and that is just the point. It requires strength, bravery, fortitude, and endurance.

That said, Keats turns in the final stanza to metaphysical reflection. From physician, the voice turns to truth-teller, for the beauty and the love that have been embraced and advanced, do not last. Melancholy *will* set in. The culprit is, again, change and mutability. The opening verses represent a contradiction of *Endymion*'s with its confident assurance that "A thing of beauty is a joy for ever." Here: "She dwells with Beauty— Beauty that must die;/And Joy, whose hand is ever at his lips/Bidding adieu; and aching Pleasure nigh,/Turning to poison while the bee-mouth sips." Beauty and joy do not, then, pace *Endymion*, remain twined in blithe opposition to mutability, almost interchangeable; indeed, they remain together, but now precisely as victims alike of change: "Ay, in the very temple of Delight/Veil'd Melancholy has her Sovran shrine,/ Though seen of none save him whose strenuous tongue/Can burst Joy's grape against his palate fine." Only the soul of such a person "shall taste the sadness of her might,/And be among her cloudy trophies hung." Delight and melancholy are inseparable, says Keats: the responsible poet.

The structure inherent in this understanding is akin (at least) to Eliot's. In his most famous poem, the wastelanders seek the very thing that will insure their death: the water they and the land lack, the water that the "famous clairvoyante" Madame Sosostris warns them to fear, and the forgotten title of the fourth part, "Death by Water." Whereas, that is, Keats links melancholy and joy, the wastelanders separate them, failing to understand that the way "out" lies precisely in the way in, through, and by means of that which they earnestly seek—for Eliot, fire is the way to "the rose": "to be restored, our sickness must grow worse" and "If to be warmed, then I must freeze/And quake in frigid, purgatorial fires" ("East Coker").

Eliot and Keats are both concerned with ideas, obviously, but Eliot the poet is always also Eliot the philosopher. For Keats, the reigning essential structure of thought that opposes simple polar oppositions serves to help us understand basic human emotions and passions

"Ode to a Nightingale" is one of Keats's best-known and most revered poems. It is dramatic in a way and to an extent that we have not before encountered in the Odes. For the first time as well, the speaker himself—who, again, is not to be identified with Keats—is involved in the action of the poem. There is a narrative here, however slight, over eight stanzas, and uncomplicated; it proceeds from the poet's attraction to the nightingale and its beguiling song.

Hugh Kenner has written with characteristic helpfulness of this poem:

> Keats is establishing certain obvious connections between the
> nightingale and the poet. His emotional adventures in this poem
> are prompted partly by the nightingale's prestige (see stanza 7),
> which in turn is connected with the Greek legend about how she got her
> voice. She was originally a maiden named Philomela. Tereus raped
> her and removed her tongue so she could make no accusations.
> Transformed into a bird, she pours forth her woes in song, which
> of course no one understands clearly.[8]

Kenner helps us recall Eliot's treatment of Philomela in *The Waste Land*. In any case, as helpful as the critic is here, he goes awry, I believe, in assuming an identity between the speaker in Keats's poem and Keats himself, outside the poem.

The poem opens with the represented poet's words about himself: "My heart aches." It is as if, he says, he had drunk hemlock or "emptied some dull opiate to the drains," so that, by whatever means, he had sunk "Lethe-wards." The poet is actually happy—"too happy"—and not at all envious in listening to the happiness of the nightingale, singing "of summer in full-throated ease."

Strangely, or so it seems, the poet now reverses himself and wishes for "a draught of vintage" with its embodiment of "a long age in the deep-delved earth,/Tasting of Flora and the country green,/Dance, and Provencal song, and sunburnt mirth." Or else, he goes on, he wishes "for a beaker full of the warm South,/Full of the true, the blushful Hippocrene, /With beaded bubbles winking at the brim,/And purple-stained mouth." Then he "might drink, and leave the world unseen," and with the nightingale "fade away into the forest dim." Keats relies on adjectives, for he describes, rather than observes, and he is intent on *painting pictures*.

The poet inside the poem is not a *character*, but a *pole of thematic action*. Less so than the speaker in a Browning or an Eliot dramatic monologue is the speaker in Keats's Odes the recipient of the reader's judgment;[9] rather, he is the means by which, in the case of "Ode to a Nightingale," escape and acceptance, temptation and resistance, are represented and treated. The speaker is, in other words, less an agent than a literary device, even though he is a poet himself. What matters, after all, is not him but the ideas. And that seems odd to say in treating a Romantic poet, and especially one so often in the past accused of being "a versifying pet-lamb" whose poems "mean next to nothing."[10] In "Ode to a Nightingale," attention is trained on what the bird represents—that is, ideas surrounding the bird—and how the poet-speaker responds to those ideas or themes. But—and this is worth emphasizing—this is no realistic or naturalistic situation; it is fictive, deliberately insisting on its own fictive nature, in fact.

Following the first two stanzas, with their opening (metaphorical) declaration that "My heart aches," and with the accompanying acknowledgment that feels as if the speaker has indulged in hemlock or "some dull opiate," and then the lament for "a draught of vintage" with *its* promise of escape from the "world" with the nightingale, the poet continues. Indeed, the third stanza is a close continuation of the previous. He would "Fade far away, dissolve, and quite forget/What thou among the leaves hast never known." He proceeds to describe what knowledge of the world entails, and he does so in such terms as a physician might use—Keats sharply identifies the condition we share, including the ravages of time upon the body: "The weariness, the fever, and the fret/Here, where men sit and hear each other groan,/Where palsy shakes a few, sad, last gray hairs,/Where youth grows pale, and spectre-thin, and dies" and pointedly, "Where but to think is to be full of sorrow/And leaden-eyed despairs." This place we inhabit, he says, is also "Where Beauty cannot keep her lustrous eyes,/Or new Love pine at them beyond to-morrow." The poet-physician also identifies other maladies inherent in the human condition (not unlike the speaker encountering the "familiar compound ghost" in Eliot's "Little Gidding"). The enemy is time: in Keats, time the destroyer is not, pace Eliot, also time the preserver.

Given these "circumstances," and this condition, the poet opts to join the nightingale. But the means he now chooses is not "Bacchus and his pards" but "the viewless wings of Poesy" (why "viewless," I wonder, coming from Eliot as I do). And indeed, "there is no light" as the poet finds himself immediately with the nightingale. Without light, the poet cannot see the (imagined) flowers nor the "soft incense." He is thus deprived of a whole named host of beautiful natural delights, ending with "mid-May's eldest child,/The coming musk-rose, full of dewy wine,/The murmurous haunt of flies on summer eves." Dare I ask how, since he cannot see them, the poet knows the various *flora* abound where he is? I understand that the poet is deep in imagination here, but even so the question looms.

Unable to see, the represented poet listens, and as he does so, he confesses that, indeed, "for many a time/I have been half in love with easeful Death." Now, thanks to the bird, death seems all the more attractive: "Now more than ever seems it rich to die, /To cease upon the midnight with no pain,/While thou art pouring forth thy soul abroad,/In such an ecstasy!" Suddenly, the last two verses of the stanza take a different, probably unexpected turn, as the speaker realizes a difference between himself and the nightingale, between his situation and the nightingale's, for his is marked by inescapable, inevitable mutability and impending death: "Still wouldst thou sing, and I have ears in vain—/To thy high requiem become a sod." This last, rather unpoetic word is perfect (as was "glut" in "Psyche"), recalling the speaker to earth.

In the penultimate stanza, the speaker muses on the nightingale's immortality: "Thou wast not born for death." The voice of the bird has been heard in ancient times and Biblical: "The same that oft-times hath/Charm'd magic casements, opening on the foam/Of perilous seas, in faery lands forlorn." Difference does not, then, attach to the nightingale, nor mutability.

The present-ness of the poem—the simultaneity of the speaking and the event, in other words, of the represented action and the representation—is fulfilled in the beginning of the final stanza, which proceeds from the reverberating last word of the previous stanza: "Forlorn! The very word is like a bell/To toll me back from thee to my sole self!" The speaker realizes that he has been in thrall to "fancy" and its attractive, indeed seductive, weavings: "Adieu!," he says, "The fancy cannot cheat so well/As she is fam'd to do, deceiving elf." Then he avers, beginning by saying again: "Adieu! Adieu! Thy plaintive anthem fades/Past the near meadows, over the still stream,/Up the hill-side; and now 'tis buried deep/In the next valley-glades." The last two verses have the well-known questioning: "Was it a vision, or a waking dream? /Fled is that music:—Do I wake or sleep?" This end is not thematic but rhetorical.

For comparison of "Nightingale" with an Eliot poem, I turn, not to *The Waste Land* as mentioned earlier, nor to "East Coker," but to the treatment of the thrush (sometimes the hermit-thrush) near the beginning of "Burnt Norton." I refer to the scene in which the bird serves as escort into a Garden that resembles the Garden in Eden. The bird is problematic, albeit in ways different from Keats's nightingale. In the Ode, the nightingale is associated with another temptation, alluring, promising, seductive, its song melodious and glorious (as the poet wishes his would be). In Eliot's drama, the thrush is explicitly cited for its "deception," a notion not at all foreign to "Nightingale" in which, however, the bird is not the agent of deception, which is, instead, the very imaginative capacity that has gripped the poet-speaker with the vision and the reflections stemming from that vision: "Adieu! The fancy cannot cheat so well/As she is fam'd to do, deceiving elf."

In "Burnt Norton," the bird urges "us" on, directing us, if not rushing us, into the brilliantly imagined Garden:

> Quick, said the bird, find them,
> Round the corner. Through the first gate,
> Into our first world, shall we follow
> The deception of the thrush? Into our first world.

The thrice-mentioned "first" well establishes that the scene is (somehow) related to our "genesis" according to the Biblical account. That this is our "first world" imaginatively rendered is also clear, and that means, despite what the thrush would, apparently, have us believe, namely that we are witnesses to the historical event itself, that the ensuing scene is not real—it is, though, "actual." The point is confirmed near the end of the scene when the deceiving thrush says: "Go, go, go . . . /human kind/Cannot bear very much reality." It is the ontologically and metaphysically "real" that the scene dramatizes, not (for Christians) the empirically verifiable scene that the Garden in Eden denominates.

The "fancy" that Keats refers to as cheating and deceiving appears in *Four Quartets* as a mistake in the way of seeing and understanding. The imagined scene there is not to be dismissed, but neither is it to be taken literally. The thrush would have us see the scene simply as "real," but it is, as I said, "actual": that is, the "actual" is the truth revealed in the scene. What the "fancy" seizes as truth, according to Keats in "Nightingale," is deception.

I find the shorter "Ode on a Grecian Urn" very appealing, indeed. Partly because it is tighter; partly because there is no "I" here, whose similarities to and differences from Keats himself have to be negotiated around troubled waters, shoals, and determined and menacing interpretive creatures. The poem focuses a beautiful work of art, pottery, not a song sung, however sweetly, by a bird. The questions posed to the urn lead to reflections, but they are born of close, intense observation of a material object perceived *in* the world, not clouded by possible dreams nor considered in the represented miasma of opiates and other drugs. There is, that is, no space given to other forms of escape, which shines the spotlight squarely on the art-object. Nor is there, for it is unnecessary, any time or poetic energy spent on conditions in the world that make the Urn seem necessary. "Ode on a Grecian Urn" is magnificently restrained.

Not at all melodramatic, "Ode on a Grecian Urn" is also more realistic than "Ode to a Nightingale," the plot similar, of course, but simpler. Death is not directly stated, the poem instead powerfully suggestive. It opens on the note of the Urn's immutability, no time or words wasted: "Thou still unravish'd bride of quietness,/Thou foster-child of silence and slow time, /Sylvan historian, who canst thus express/A flowery tale more sweetly than our rhyme." Then follow a series of seven questions, with which the first of five stanzas concludes. The questions have to do with the representations on the Urn. As it happens, Eliot's "Burnt Norton" employs the same imagery in confronting the challenge posed by words themselves, their changeableness, their refusal to "stay still," and their liability to abuse and misuse:

> Only by the form, the pattern,
> Can words or music reach
> The stillness, as a Chinese jar still
> Moves perpetually in its stillness.
> Not the stillness of the violin, while the note lasts,
> Not that only, but the co-existence....

Eliot thus invokes—characteristically proceeding by means of comparison—the "sister arts" of music and pottery in order to challenge deleterious changeableness. Shortly thereafter, Eliot adds, "The detail of the pattern is movement." The crux of his offering is captured in the last word I just quoted: "co-existence."

The second stanza of Keats's great poem is addressed to the figures on the Urn, human and inanimate. The speaker now focuses on the lack of change in the youth and the girl. Opposite to Eliot, Keats thus sees stasis and stillness (only). True, the "Bold Lover" can never kiss, "Though winning near the goal," but, says the speaker, "do not grieve;/She cannot fade, though thou hast not thy bliss,/For ever wilt thou love, and she be fair!" The next stanza expands on these thematic observations, and ends, just barely reminding us of the physician at work, with the contrast between "happy, happy love," and (inferior) "human passion," which "leaves a heart high-sorrowful and cloy'd,/A burning forehead, and a parching tongue" (thus echoing "La Belle Dame sans Merci").

With the penultimate stanza, questions return, this time three. The scene on the Urn represents people coming to a sacrifice, with a "mysterious priest" leading the "heifer lowing at the skies." "What little town by river or sea shore," asks the speaker, "Or mountain-built with peaceful citadel,/Is emptied of this folk, this pious morn"? It is thus not just the represented scene that the speaker reflects on, but, as if the scene were live and true, in other words "real" rather than "actual," also the "deep" story of the figures appearing on the Urn, whose very silence allows these thoughts to form and then surface, emerging. Keats thus gets inside the represented figures, feeling as they do, indeed at-one with them in an act of intense sympathetic engagement.

The final stanza opens with an address directly to the Urn as "Thou," whose "silent form, dost tease us out of thought/As doth eternity: Cold Pastoral!" Teasing us out of thought could be a good thing, but that is not at all what Keats means here. "Cold Pastoral" is a striking judgment, particularly in relation to the represented scenes on the Urn, which matter most. The Urn is beautiful, no question about that, but the beauty that Keats is interested in is inseparable from the truth told in and by the representation.

Thus come the final five verses, with the implicit ambiguity about who says what, but first a declaration of the Urn's usefulness in providing needed solace and comfort: "When old age shall this generation waste,/Thou shalt remain, in midst of other woe/Than ours, a friend to man," unchanging and (so) always present and available for consolation. To us, the Urn says, in fact, "'Beauty is truth, truth beauty,'—that is all/Ye know on earth, and all ye need to know." I believe it matters less where the quotation marks go than so many scholars and critics have supposed. That is, as long as we are clear about the meanings of the words, especially "Truth" and "Beauty," which we have seen, appear elsewhere in Keats and constitute a perennial concern, particularly their relations. Truth *is* beauty—as long as we understand that by "truth" is meant the kind that involves the poem's reader in active negotiation. No one, least of all John Keats, believes that everything true is beautiful, but the truth that the "Ode on a Grecian Urn" represents via responsible reading is not so simple; its truth is, in fact, that the "Cold Pastoral" does not, as object, give us truth. The truth lies, as we have seen, in the reader's intersection with the poem itself and, behind that, the speaker's imaginative reconstruction of the scene and her or his reflection on that which is there represented.

"Ode on a Grecian Urn" thus appears to take a more complex approach than Eliot's to the nature of artistic representation. Eliot's focus is, after all, narrower, although not reductive, dealing with the building-blocks that are words. The Modernist poet's interest lies principally with the story—and the narrative truth—told by the comparisons made of language, music, and pottery. It is the over-riding structural matter of "co-existence" that he wishes us to arrive at. What interests Keats is not the Urn as piece of pottery, that is, the beauty of that shaping, its form, but the *story* represented on it and, indeed, the figures who people that representation. He cares most about human response, about available consolation to change and suffering—and, above all else, to the truth that beauty holds and reveals. For him, the figures on the Urn may as well be real.

"To Autumn," last of the Odes, a poem finally giving that season its due, consists of but three stanzas, each of 11 verses. The poem is markedly different from the other Odes, in addition to lacking that genre-word in the title, that is. Keats's poetic strategy in these 33 taut lines is both indirect and sophisticated. The poem continues in the objectivist mode of "Ode on a Grecian Urn," but it features only three questions, and at least two of these appear more emphatic than rhetorical. There is again, as in "Ode on a Grecian Urn," no "I," and less reflection even than there. That the new poem is *to* Autumn signals an intimacy, such as "Nightingale" exploits.

The most significant thematic difference lies in the way that "To Autumn" lacks any temptation toward escape; neither poet nor reader is drawn to the poem's subject in a way that must ultimately be rejected, despite all the attraction and the sweetness and the promise of the temptation. Here, Keats takes as subject neither an abstraction nor an animate "object," but a topic that, as the third stanza makes quite clear, does not come trailing garlands of poetic fancy, nor, indeed, a history of poetic attention. The "point," although it does not seem to matter as much as point does in the other Odes, is simply that Autumn "hast thy music too." The slightest suggestion inheres, albeit very indirectly, that the words of these magnificent verses relate to and bear on the seasons of human life, as well. Still, Autumn is hardly a mere metaphor.

What it is, is the fullest expression we have of Keats's humanity: not, of course, because the poem is his consummate, lyric expression of the wonders of later "life." It is not at all that; far from it. Here, Keats captures the season; he does not exude, reflect, or lament. He gives us the effects of Autumn, characterizes her in human terms, and then moves out to (earned) commentary. Keats literally *embodies* Autumn, and in so doing reveals a human and artistic response in one and the same wondrous act. Keats aptly wrote the following, in a letter, regarding the poem's composition and his own point of view regarding autumn: "I never liked stubble fields so much as now—Aye, better than the chilly green of the spring. Somehow a stubble plain looks warm—in the same way that some pictures look warm—this struck me so much in my Sunday's walk that I composed upon it."[11] There is no similarity, let it be said immediately and directly, to the wastelanders' turning upside-down of the values of spring and (for them) winter. Autumn does not represent, or entail a desire for, escape (or transcendence).

The first stanza of "To Autumn" is artistically masterful. The season is first described, which Keats does with verbs and past participles reflective of growth and development. It is, as the first verse states, "Season of mists and mellow fruitfulness." Even the decision to omit the definite article before "Season" is strategic, for it is precisely the idea of "season" and with it "seasoning" that "To Autumn" is all about. The remainder, then, of the first stanza:

> Close bosom-friend of the maturing sun;
> Conspiring with him how to load and bless
>   With fruit the vines that round the thatch-eves run;
> To bend with apples the moss'd cottage-trees,
>   And fill all fruit with ripeness to the core;
>   To swell the gourd, and plump the hazel shells
> With a sweet kernel; to set budding more,
>   And still more, later flowers for the bees,
>   Until they think warm days will never cease,
>   For Summer has o'er-brimmed their clammy cells.

Autumn has done this work, active and productive. Hugh Kenner alerted me—way back in college, now more than 50 years ago—that "the rhyme scheme in stanza 1 differs from that of the other two; also the scheme of indention. One element Keats is working with is the time one feels has elapsed between rhymes. Between 'trees' (line 5) and 'bees' (line 9), there occur not only four full lines but also seven phrasal divisions, hence a sense of crowded activity."[12]

We move, as Kenner further notes, from fruit in the first stanza, to harvesting in the second, and on to stubble in the third and last. What Kenner does not note is that, as I have mentioned, the second stanza is also about the embodiment of Autumn, now represented in human terms. Here, the poet speaks to her, without, however, addressing her; he does this, though, without her in his immediate sight: he imagines Autumn as being seen, and observed, "sitting careless," elsewhere "sound asleep," "And sometimes like a gleaner thou dost keep/Steady thy laden head across a brook,/Or by a cider-press, with patient look,/Thou watchest the last oozings hours by hours." Autumn is thus both pacific and engaged, restful and active. Embodiment is a creation of imagination.

The final stanza proceeds to address Autumn herself, for the first time. In doing so, the poet shows his concern for her feelings. Unlike, then, in poems set in spring-time, where speakers complain endlessly and extravagantly upon (as it were) *les belles dames sans merci*, the poet in "To Autumn" is not at all concerned with himself. Autumn has its own consolations, the poem concludes, and they deserve our recognition. A variation on the *ubi sunt?* theme, "To Autumn" differs as day from night from "*ou sont les neiges d'antan?*" ("where are the snows of yesteryear?"). Here, the songs of spring are no longer heard—having given way to mutability—but that is no cause of alarm, lament, dismay, or despair: "Where are the songs of Spring? Ay, where are they?/Think not of them, thou hast thy music too":

> While barred clouds bloom the soft-dying day,
>   And touch the stubble-plains with rosy hue;
> Then in a wailful choir the small gnats mourn
>   Among the river sallows, borne aloft
>   Or sinking as the light wind lives or dies;
> And full-grown lambs loud bleat from hilly bourn;
>   Hedge-crickets sing; and now with treble soft
> The red-breast whistles from a garden-croft;
>   And gathering swallows twitter in the skies.

Keats leaves no doubt that winter is coming, and soon. That he refuses to say anything but what is true makes the consolations all the more believable and acceptable. We leave "To Autumn" feeling grateful. But that is not all.

The last of the Odes is the most sharply and emphatically immanentist of the six. No transcendent power can be discerned or felt in "To Autumn," and so no intersection of the timeless with time, of immutability with change (for this, compare Eliot in the opening verse paragraph of "Little Gidding," with its brilliant rendering of "Midwinter spring." Eliot goes on, further-more, to declare, and juxtapose, "maytime" with "May," thus emphasizing that *the way of seeing is all.*) Curiously, or so it would seem, Keats is the less imaginative, that is, in privileging imaginative capacity, even as he directly represents his subject as the creation of imagination in the middle stanza. Truth, for Keats here, lies not so much in a way of seeing as in the observed truth. That truth is purely immanent, in and of the things seen. Philosophy is not needed; unclouded vision is, such as we all are given. Imagination is, we may say therefore, at-one with the actual.

NOTES

1. See, esp., my *T.S. Eliot's Christmas Poems: An Essay in Writing-as-Reading and Other "Impossible Unions"* (New York: Palgrave Macmillan, 2014).

2. John Keats, *Selected Poems and Letters*, ed. Douglas Bush (Boston: Riverside-Houghton Mifflin, 1959).

3. T.S. Eliot, *Four Quartets* (New York: Harcourt, Brace, 1943).

4. Eliot, *Ash-Wednesday: Six Poems* (London: Faber and Faber, 1930).

5. Quoted in John Keats, *Selected Poems and Letters*, ed. Douglas Bush (Boston, MA: Riverside-Houghton Mifflin, 1959), 346. The preceding quotaion from Keats regarding "Psyche" is also taken from 346.

6. Walter Jackson Bate, *The Stylistic Development of Keats* (New York: Humanities Press, 1945).

7. The image is prominent in Eliot, including in *Ash-Wednesday: Six Poems* and *Four Quartets.*

8. Hugh Kenner, *The Art of Poetry* (New York: Holt, Rinehart and Winston, 1961), 300–1.

9. See Robert Langbaum's classic study *The Poetry of Experience: The Dramatic Monologue in Modern Literary Tradition* (New York: Random House, 1957).

10. Keats, letter to Miss Jeffrey, 9 June 1819; see William Michael Rossetti, *Life of John Keats* (London, 1887), 183.

11. Keats, *Selected Poems and Letters*, 359.

12. Kenner, *The Art of Poetry*, 274.

CHAPTER 4

Fleeing into the Storm: Beauty and Truth in "The Eve of St. Agnes"

Abstract This chapter consists of a long section, composed of a slightly revised version of an article first published in 1973, and a brief addendum, sketching a possible new reading controversial in both argument and approach. The earlier section challenges previous commentary, especially Jack Stillinger's. Instead of a "skeptical" representation of a "hoodwinked" heroine and a rapist protagonist, "The Eve of St. Agnes" is a carefully "framed" story of intense love, the hero "saved" by the faith and goodness of the heroine. The poem provides "consolation," as "a thing of beauty"; at the same time, Keats the responsible poet, truth-teller, and "physician" insures that his reader neither take the story as "real" nor assume that complete, lasting happiness exists.

Keyword Revision of earlier article · Addendum · Sketching a possible new reading · Poem as consolation · Poet as truth-teller

> And they are gone: ay, ages long ago
> These lovers fled away into the storm.
>
> —"The Eve of St. Agnes"
>
> The end is where we start from.
>
> —T.S. Eliot, "Little Gidding," in *Four Quartets*

The ending of "The Eve of St. Agnes" leaves little to the imagination and little room for doubt regarding the fate of its characters, all of them, in fact.

© The Author(s) 2016
G.D. Atkins, *On Keats's Practice and Poetics of Responsibility*,
DOI 10.1007/978-3-319-44144-3_4

The realistic tenor of this, the 42nd, stanza stands in striking contrast to the high-romantic nature of the plot and the exquisite beauty, sensuous and sensual, of many of its tableaux. A frame thus surrounds Keats's take on the Romeo-and-Juliet story. In fact, the ending directly returns the reader to the opening stanza, which doubles-down on the cold of St. Agnes' Eve (January 20). "The Eve of St. Agnes" works, achieving its greatest effects, by means of comparison and contrast.[1]

The Christian Beadsman, who is the last character mentioned in the poem, is also the first we see, confirming the existence of a frame and signifying the importance of the Beadsman's asceticism in the poem's overall architecture and thematic—specifically anti-Christian—drive and direction. A figure largely from pre-Reformation times, a Beadsman was a special servant, a pensioner, one whose duty it was to pray for his benefactor.

> St. Agnes' Eve—Ah, bitter chill it was!
> The owl, for all his feathers, was a-cold;
> The hare limp'd trembling through the frozen grass;
> And silent was the flock in woolly fold:
> Numb were the Beadsman's fingers, while he told
> His rosary, and while his frosted breath,
> Like pious incense from a censer old,
> Seem'd taking flight for heaven, without a death,
> Past the sweet Virgin's picture, while his prayer he saith.

The Spenserian stanzas are abetted in creating a medieval "feel" by the frequent archaisms. The Beadsman, by the way, continues to function into the fourth stanza—"His was harsh penance on St. Agnes' Eve," taking a way in direct contrast with the riotous, violent, and materialistic revelers at party.

Keats spends what may seem an inordinate amount of space and time on the Beadsman, for he is to contrast not just with the revelers, the Baron's "hyena foemen," as the narrator of "The Eve of St. Agnes" calls them. As much as that narrator dislikes these men, while liking, and siding with, Porphyro, he seems tempered and balanced regarding the Beadsman, treating him with no disrespect, despite Keats's views of Christianity especially as expressed in the Letters, but yet letting us know of his unnecessary sacrifices and ineffectualness—all in all, a generous enough representation: "His prayer he saith, this patient, holy man;/Then takes his lamp, and riseth from his knees,/And back returneth, meagre, barefoot, wan,/Along the chapel aisle by slow degrees." The scene Keats paints is correspondingly cold, with the significant role here played by ineffectual art hardly serving as mediating beauty or tying us to the earth, away from which everything leads that the Beadsman touches or sees: "The sculptur'd dead, on each side, seem to freeze,/Emprison'd in black, purgatorial rails:/Knights, ladies, praying in dumb orat'ries." Moreover, the Beadsman exemplifies his basic mode of being, the same as that of the art he walks past: he *bypasses*. Keats quietly emphasizes that "his weak spirit fails/To think how they may ache in icy hoods and mails." Passing by is thus passing up for the Beadsman, an avenue for further contrasts to play.

Temptations do not faze the earnest, pious Beadsman, at least not beyond a present moment:

> Northward he turneth through a little door,
> And scarce three steps, ere Music's golden tongue
> Flatter'd to tears this aged man and poor;
> But no—already had his deathbell rung:
> The joys of all his life were said and sung:
> His was harsh penance on St. Agnes' Eve:
> Another way he went, and soon among
> Rough ashes sat he for his soul's reprieve,
> And all night kept awake, for sinners' sake to grieve.

The Beadsman's life as such is essentially over and past; he seems now irrelevant. The contrast being established with others is vivid.

The title of the poem, as well as the dynamics driving the plot, refers to the night preceding the Feast Day—January 21st—of St. Agnes, the young woman martyred in fourth-century Rome, who became the patron saint of virgins. Superstition had it that, if a young woman performed certain rites and rituals on St. Agnes' Eve, she would be rewarded with a glimpse of her future husband. In the version of the superstition on which Keats drew, the petitioning girl had to retire without supper, undress herself, and enter her bed completely naked, as well as, among other things, not look behind her as she proceeded.

With the legend obviously at work, the fact of the frame surrounding the central action based in that superstition, the various contrasts employed, among them, sensuous and sensual indulgence, asceticism, and romance, it is hard to see how the Victorians could view the poem as meaning "next to nothing." It seems, on the contrary, to be highly charged with meaning.

In the twentieth century, Earl Wasserman, in a book whose title derives from Keats, *The Finer Tone*, argued, in great detail, that the poem represents a validation of the power of imagination.[2] And indeed, the young woman's romantic dream is fulfilled as she glimpses Porphyro, with whom she flees at the end. A bit later, Jack Stillinger would have none of it and wrote of Madeline's being "hoodwinked," and indeed "raped" by young Porphyro.[3] Everything I have already said, and everything I will say, has to be either ignored or else turned in textually (and biographically) unjustified directions, to come up with this still-current reading.

Following the stanzas devoted to the Beadsman, "The Eve of St. Agnes" turns to "the argent revelry," who receive barely five lines. From this point, halfway through the fifth stanza, to the end of the 41st, the focus is on the legend, Madeline, and Porphyro, with some attention given to "one old beldame, weak in body and in soul." That is Angela, whose name appears charged, and who assists, despite reservations, in Porphyro's plan to make his way through the mansion to his love's bedchamber. Framed, as we have seen, these central stanzas constitute the bulk of the poem. More "meaning" may well be packed into the framing verses—those that we have looked at—than into the 30-plus stanzas that detail Madeline's observance of the St. Agnes' Eve rites, Porphyro's elaborate setting of the scene before revealing himself to Madeline, and, finally, the dramatization of their love-making. The framed scenes carry considerable intensity, and are beautifully depicted, sensuous delights, feasts of the senses for the reader as they are for Madeline herself. To Keats, meaning matters, and greatly—thus the attention devoted to the Beadsman and the way he essentially stands for forgoing the pleasures available in the world—but still, the Victorians were onto something, after all, for the center of the poem, and by far the greater part of its length, are devoted to description and creation of pictures.

The revelers rightly receive little attention because they represent an extreme or perverted kind of romance, one that consists of apparently mindless and extravagant merry-making. It also includes prodigality, indulgent sensuality, and an obvious penchant for violence—Keats by no

means hides the "romance" character of the scene he is painting, the story
he is weaving:

> At length burst in the argent revelry,
> With plume, tiara, and rich array,
> Numerous as the shadows haunting fairily
> The brain, new stuff'd, in youth, with triumphs gay
> Of old romance. These let us wish away. . . .

In stanza 10, the narrator is less restrained, representing the Baron and
his minions, reprobates all, in no uncertain terms, as we encounter the
hero Porphyro for the first time: "He ventures in: let no buzz'd whisper
tell:/All eyes be muffled, or a hundred swords/Will storm his heart,
Love's fev'rous citadel." In these medieval halls, which Keats labels as
"that mansion foul," are nothing but "barbarian hordes,/Hyena foemen, and hot-blooded lords"; their "very dogs would execrations
howl/Against his lineage." There is, however, one exception—and,
pointedly, it is not the Beadsman, who would afford him "any mercy,"
no one "Save one old beldame, weak in body and in soul."

This is no Montagues-versus-Capulets redivvus; the situation is
more dire, the evil—and it is that in "The Eve of St. Agnes"—
unevenly divided. Angela echoes the narrator, referring to "the whole
blood-thirty race" and then continuing with the following plea to
Porphyro, whom she assists and whom she fervently seeks to protect:
"Get hence! Get hence!" she pleads. She then proceeds to detail two
of the worst of the "barbarians." "Alas me!" she repeats, "flit!/Flit like
a ghost away."

The narrator, whose judgment of the revelers and the Baron and his
henchmen we have already observed, favors Porphyro, and seems somewhat equivocal toward Madeline. Indeed, he describes her initially as
"thoughtful" but "Full of this whim," that is, the legend of St. Agnes'
Eve. Porphyro, at the same time, the narrator would assist, Angela-like:
"He ventures in: let no buzz'd whisper tell:/All eyes be muffled." To be
sure, the narrator scrupulously acknowledges the thought—and its carnal
nature—that pops quickly into Porphyro's head upon hearing from
Angela the details of Madeline's commitment to the legend. In fact,
Porphyro proposes "A stratagem, that makes the beldame start." She
exclaims: "A cruel man and impious thou art." Of Madeline, she says,
"Sweet lady, let her pray, and sleep, and dream/Alone with her good

angels, far apart/From wicked men like thee." Angela adds: "Go, go!—I deem/Thou canst not surely be the same that thou didst seem."

In return, Porphyro pledges that he intends no harm to the young woman dreaming, and Angela immediately feels reassured and, almost as quickly, wrings from him "gentler speech": "Ah! Why wilt thou affright a feeble soul?/A poor, weak, palsy-stricken, churchyard thing,/Whose prayers for thee, each morn and evening,/Were never miss'd." The change in Porphyro is immediate, and great, perhaps attributable, finally, to mystery: "A gentler speech from burning Porphyro,/So woful, and of such deep sorrowing,/That Angela gives promise she will do/Whatever he shall wish, betide her weal or woe." She thus effectively becomes both Porphyro's and Madeline's guardian *angel*, and, as well, his necessary intermediary. The following words follow immediately those I have just now quoted, leaving no doubt as to the nature of Porphyro's burning desire *or* of his ultimately honorable intentions as they spell out Angela's plan, "Which was, to lead him, in close secrecy,/Even to Madeline's chamber, and there hide/Him in a closet, of such privacy/That he might see her beauty unespied," and that special, dream-haunted night "win perhaps . . . a peerless bride."

The stanza ends with another statement placing this story in the context of other *stories*: "Never on such a night have lovers met, /Since Merlin paid his Demon all the monstrous debt." In other words, the story of Madeline and Porphyro, Angela and the Beadman, and Hildebrand and Maurice and the Baron—the story is of the same nature as the legend to which Madeline pledged fealty. And it too promises to save—as long as you do not misconstrue it as anything other than a work of the (literary) imagination.

Angela pledges that "It shall be as thou wishest," promising, in fact, to make available "All cates and dainties" for "this feast-night." Not long thereafter, she returns and guides Porphyro to Madeline's chamber, as he had implored of her, and the narrative now turns a rosy-hued light on the heroine, bathed in religious terms: "Madeline, St. Agnes' charmed maid,/Rose, like a mission'd spirit, unaware." As Angela guides Porphyro along, the narrator interjects, addressing him directly, and seconding the old "beldame's" actions: "Now prepare,/Young Porphyro, for gazing on that bed,/She comes, she comes again, like ring-dove fray'd and fled."

The following scenes, lavishly represented, are sensuous delights—for the characters and readers alike. *"We"* are very much in the story, like the narrator, who is like both Porphyro and Angela. The description is elaborate, over-extended, and, if not gratuitous, thematically extravagant; it is, in other words, *there* for reasons other than theme, other than necessity:

> A casement high and triple-arch'd there was,
> All garlanded with carven imag'ries
> Of fruits, and flowers, and bunches of knot-grass,
> And diamonded with panes of quaint device,
> Innumerable of stains and splendid dyes,
> As are the tiger-moth's deep-damask'd wings;
> And in the midst, 'mong thousand heraldries,
> And twilight saints, and dim emblazonings,
> A shielded scutcheon blush'd with blood of queens and kings.

The carven images conspire with the present feast being laid out, one thing mirroring another.

Immediately follows—directly linked with the foregoing stanza—an equally elaborate description of Madeline herself, bathed as she is in the soft rose of the moon's light and represented in terms deeply religious: so pure does she appear, in her (soon-to-be) nakedness, that Porphyro is shaken.

> Full on this casement shone the wintry moon,
> And threw warm gules on Madeline's fair breast,
> As down she knelt for heaven's grace and boon;
> Rose-bloom fell on her hands, together prest,
> And on her silver cross soft amethyst,
> And on her hair a glory, like a saint:
> She seem'd a splendid angel, newly drest,
> Save wings, for heaven:—Porphyro grew faint:
> She knelt, so pure a thing, so free from mortal taint.

The next stanza continues the physical description of Madeline, her hair now free, "her fragrant boddice" loosened and then slowly let fall to her knees. Once in bed, she is said to be "Blissfully haven'd both from joy and pain;/Clasp'd like a missal where swart Paynims pray;/Blinded alike from sunshine and from rain,/As though a rose should shut, and be a bud again"—very suggestive phrasing, indeed. Porphyro, meanwhile, is said to have "Stol'n to this paradise."

Then, while she sleeps, Porphyro sets a sumptuous table. Speaking to her for the first time, he whispers: "'And now, my love, my seraph fair, awake!/Thou art my heaven, and I thine eremite:/Open thine eyes, for meek St. Agnes' sake, /Or I shall drowse beside thee, so my soul doth ache.'" In two previous versions of this essay on "The Eve of St. Agnes," I have argued that the frequent and bold religious language, alongside other textual and biographical facts, lead to the probability that Keats meant the poem to dramatize a *religion of love*, an(other) alternative, and perhaps a "grander" one, than the Christian religion affords.[4] That may well be the case; I am not willing to back away from the claims. After all, other of Keats's poems make the point, including "Ode to Fanny" ("Let none profane my Holy See of love,/Or with a rude hand break/The sacramental cake," a sonnet to Fanny ("as I've read love's missal through to-day,/He'll let me sleep, seeing I fast and pray"), and, probably most important, a letter to Fanny Brawne in late 1819: "I could be martyr'd for my Religion—Love is my religion—I could die for that. I could die for you. My Creed is Love and you are its only tenet. You have ravish'd me away by a Power I cannot resist."[5] But now I do not think we have to presuppose anything quite so systematic on Keats's part. For it is not religion that matters. What matters, rather, is what has been experienced, which bears, in taking the place of conventional religion, religious significance.

In any case, Madeline continues her dreaming, even as Porphyro tries sweetly to awaken her. On her lute he plays "an ancient ditty, long since mute,/In Provence called 'La belle dame sans mercy.'" Suddenly, her eyes open, Madeline "still beheld.../...the vision of her sleep." Now the dream is realized, embodied, in fact, and immediately we read: "There was a painful change." It is so strong that it "nigh expell'd/ The blisses of her dream so pure and deep." At this, Madeline began to weep and to "mourn forth witless words with many a sigh." Still, though, her gaze remains on Porphyro "Who knelt, with joined hands and piteous eye,/Fearing to move or speak, she look'd so dreamingly." The difference, inevitable, unavoidable, between dreaming and living in the real world thus powerfully asserts itself, no matter if the reality is a fulfillment of the dream—perhaps a "doubtful" tale from faery land, as "Lamia" puts it, "hard for the non-elect to understand" (2.6). What happens then, after Madeline remarks on "How chang'd thou art," fulfills what Keats said about the situation depicted: I would not, he averred, be such "an eunuch in sentiment" as to leave such a maiden unsatisfied.[6] So: "Into her dream he melted, as the rose/Blendeth its odour with the violet,—/Solution sweet." Pointedly, as the sexual union proceeds, the outside breaks in: "the frost-wind blows/Like Love's alarum pattering the sharp sleet/Against the window panes." Now "St. Agnes' moon hath set."

Porphyro has some convincing to do, although Madeline seems already lost in the reality he represents. At any rate, the terms he uses are again palpably religious. In fact, the 38th stanza contains the most important, overtly religious language in "The Eve of St. Agnes." I find no justification for questioning Porphyro's sincerity here: if—and I emphasize *if*—he could be faulted at the beginning of his journey through that "mansion foul," when, perhaps, he was simply burning with physical desire, now he seems to have had that desire purified into love that Eliot defines in "Little Gidding." That does not mean transcendence of physical desire; obviously, Porphyro, and Madeline as well, are happy with physical expressions of love. In other words, however scantily it has been represented, and however quickly a significant change has occurred, Porphyro's has been a version of the "journey toward understanding."[7] Love occurs and is expressed *in* the physical.

In a romance that works hard to insure that the reader never consider it otherwise than as a romance, it is perfectly appropriate, and indeed likely, that events will transpire that exceed a realistic time frame and a naturalistic version of human psychology. Here is the 38th stanza:

> "My Madeline! Sweet dreamer! Lovely bride!
> Say, may I be for aye thy vassal blest?
> Thy beauty's shield, heart-shap'd and vermeil dyed?
> Ah, silver shrine, here will I take my rest
> After so many hours of toil and quest,
> A famish'd pilgrim,—saved by miracle.
> Though I have found, I will not rob thy nest
> Saving of thy sweet self; if thou think'st well
> To trust, fair Madeline, to no rude infidel.

The claims are large, though not exaggerated or extravagant: Porphyro is proposing marriage, as he declares himself to have been "changed" by what he has happily experienced.

Perhaps indicative of his new-found sensibility, Porphyro further reassures Madeline with more-than-encouraging words regarding their escape from that "mansion foul." In fact, he turns the raging storm outside—that "circumstance"–into positive opportunity, setting the stage for the poem's most important positive statement while once again affirming the romance nature of the story itself. The storm that (potentially) benefits Madeline and Porphyro, assisting them in their escape (another striking instance of outside assistance), works against the "hyena foemen" presumably because of the latter's indulgences: "Hark! 'tis an elfin-storm from faery land,/Of haggard seeming, but a boon indeed." Possibility resides in circumstances, a positive in the negative—a soul perhaps to be made precisely out of life's terrors and horror. Since the wassaillers are dead-drunk, the young and fortunate lovers may escape to "the home" Porphyro has made for Madeline "over the southern moors."

The following stanza then reaffirms the "fantastic" character of the story, for the narrator tells us "there were sleeping dragons all around,/At glaring watch, perhaps, with ready spears." And then, the escape itself, Madeline and Porphyro "glid[ing], like phantoms," past the sleeping Porter and "the wakeful eye" of the "bloodhound," whose "sagacious eye an inmate owns," another statement of the congruence of Porphyro and an outside moral order. Then "the key turns, and the door upon its hinges groans." It is all magical, down to the key represented as turning itself, that is, *without* assistance.

And so the "lovers" escape, fleeing "into the storm," which represents a radical difference from human desire for purely happy endings and which affirms Keats's insistence on truth-telling. It *is* escape, but without any transcendence of metaphorically stormy "circumstances." On the contrary, the "lovers" flee precisely *into* problems, all the while evidently embracing the opportunities.

Keats insures that his readers be under no illusions regarding Madeline, Porphyro, and their story. It is a romance, a "faery" tale, a fictional account, and what seems a happy ending—though only for them among the characters—carries no promise of escape from "circumstances." This is truth, in other words, truth that surrounds, framing, a beauty-ful story, told in lavish language, of love winning out over determined opposition, hatred, and violence. As well, it is a story of desire purified, possibly of, in Eliotesque terms, love expanded beyond normal desire.[8] Love does not conquer all, however; "circumstances" await, abounding.

The reader needs fully to grasp that love—magnificent love—exists within a framework of truth. If joy is inseparable from melancholy, melancholy is also inseparable from joy.

Addendum January 2016, Greenville, SC.

Before leaving "The Eve of St. Agnes," I wish to offer a supplement (in the sense of both addition to and extension of the foregoing reading). I do not mean to offer a substitute for the reading now decades old in essential respects. The following paragraphs, less an interpretation or reading than the outline of direction I might take in attempting a full-scale analysis, is, simply, an addendum and as such an update of my article originally published in 1973. I have chosen not to pursue the directions I open up below because that first reading, now over 40 years old, remains necessary, and therefore has a critical role to play in this book. Its main opposition continues to reign as the preferred, indeed the pre-eminent account of "The Eve of St. Agnes." I refer to Jack Stillinger's (even older) article on "The Hoodwinking of Madeline," now twice-modified and so likely both to be available to readers and to have acquired authority with the passage of time and the repeated printings.

The outline of a reading I present here is decidedly religious in nature, and it too was inspired by T.S. Eliot, particularly his treatment of two mediators in *Ash-Wednesday*, one the "Lady of silences," that is, the Virgin Mary, the other, Her follower, the "Lady," a figure of medieval romance, where she often, including in *The Divine Comedy*, represents a path toward salvation (particularly in a mystical sexual sense).[9] These thoughts were also inspired by re-considering Stillinger's arguments, in particular with an eye toward an explanation for their longevity in spite of faulty interpretations of critical points. Perhaps Stillinger touches upon some almost primal facts in and about the poem.

In any case, the closest link between Eliot's poem and Keats's has to do precisely with the power, place, meaning, and trustworthiness of romance. "The Eve of St. Agnes," written largely during January of 1819, at the beginning of his "annus mirabilis" and thus preceding the outpouring of poems of the coming Spring, reflects, as we have seen, Keats's intense interest, manifested in the letters, in the potential salvific power of love, the prominence of suffering alongside earthly consolation, and possible "schemes of salvation" (different from that promulgated and maintained by the "pious frauds" of Christianity). The poem may, in fact, be read as a retelling of the Biblical account of the Fall, which occurred, according to Genesis, in the Garden of Eden. In Keats's poem, the Edenic character is purely earthly, sensuous and sensual, and lies essentially in the sumptuous delights that the young Porphyro sets out to assist in his fulfillment of the dreams of the maid Madeline. Structurally, the male protagonist thus occupies the position of the snake. Madeline subscribes to the superstition that, if she successively performs certain acts on St. Agnes' Eve, she will attain sight of the man intended to be her husband. The Eve (of St. Agnes) is itself, then, the structural manifestation of Adam's female friend; in other words, the night is the means to and avenue of this purely secular recalling of the Fall. The Eve(ning), not "Eve," is the instrument of whatever re-interpreted Fall occurs.

The male-figure is, then, not seduced; rather, although he is not the rapist that Stillinger postulates, he is the serpent winding his way through the backstairs to Madeline's bed-chamber, led by the angel, the old Angela. In fact, the story has no Adam, and the only Eve is the night of January 20. The idea of a *fall* is likewise radically reinterpreted as positive transformation (not at all transfiguration), with sex itself become love of more than ephemeral nature (if less than eternal). That other "intensity" toward which, says Eliot, "we must be still and still moving" does not lie in another dimension, but in this one. Instead of a Fall, there is conversion.

The role of mediator, moreover, has been shifted to the well-named old crone, Angela, who is convinced by the " burning" young man to assist him in doing the Eve's work. Knowledge does, indeed, become his, in this case, of the carnal sort. In the course of the luxurious and sensual love-scene, Porphyro appears changed from merely a young man on fire with lust to one converted by Madeline's beauty and (Virgin-like) faith and obedience to a perspective that can only be defined in religious terms even as it is obviously shorn of doctrine or ritual conventionally Christian. In the event, and strikingly, importantly, Porphyro's "conversion" is simultaneous with success in his sexual quest.

At the end, the lovers "flee into the storm"; they are not expelled from the Garden, which is surrounded by malefactors, "villains," "hyena foemen," the narrator unceremoniously calls them, these "barbarian hordes." If these "opponents" were absent or somehow mollified, perhaps the couple could have—would have—stayed. Fleeing "into the storm" thus completes the total revision of the Edenic myth; they do not, as romance would have it, "live happily ever after," nor are they condemned to a life absent all consolations—for there has been no Fall, and they haven't fallen. That story is essentially nullified. The fate of the long-suffering, ever-faithful Beadsman attests to and confirms the ineffectualness of any such belief: he "slept for aye amid his ashes cold." There is no heaven, no life after death, no Christian salvation.

The differences from the Biblical story may well appear so numerous and profound as to call into question the interpretation I have just figured. There is, in truth, no gainsaying the differences. And yet hints are given, provoking guesses. Keats's retelling thus binds us to the earth, the narrative itself "a thing of beauty,/And a joy for ever." The poem itself is, therefore, an important part of the treatment of romance. That for-everness, moreover, stands opposed to the benighted and ineffectual story lived out—and died— by the Beadsman. That Keats gets (at least) half the story (that Incarnation names and that I have just referred to) helps account, I believe, for the "hints" that he drops throughout "The Eve of St. Agnes" regarding the Garden of Eden and the Fall. A part-iality obtains, an incompleteness, a lack of fulfillment. The hints matter, in any case, guesses justified, or so I will claim.

The new interpretation appears not so much latent as possible; it might be said to "attend" the poem as possibility. But it differs radically from Eliot's rendering of the Garden in the first part of "Burnt Norton." There, the Garden is (re-)imagined; what counts, ultimately, is the "actual-ness" of that scene, which restores "With a new verse the ancient rhyme." In other words, the Modernist poem represents a scene that may be in ways at once the Garden (of Eden) and not the Garden of Eden—an "impossible union." "Incarnation," says Eliot, is "the hint *half* guessed, the gift *half* understood" ("The Dry Salvages"; italics added).

Perhaps possibility itself assumes a place among the points that Keats wishes his reader to take away from "The Eve of St. Agnes." His sense of responsibility to truth and reality is such that he cannot quite bring himself to consummate—unlike his hero—his love for the (un-Christian) truth that the poem incarnates. Perhaps this unlikely, but possible, new interpertation can be seen as attending and shedding light on both Stillnger's and my own readings.

NOTES

1. Here, at least, for Keats, unlike Eliot, comparison amounts to contrast; it is a direct notice to the reader. For Eliot, differently, comparison carries thematic weight.
2. Earl Wasserman, *The Finer Tone: Keats' Major Poems* (Baltimore, MD: Johns Hopkins P, 1953).

3. Jack Stillinger, "The Hoodwinking of Madeline: Scepticism in 'The Eve of St. Agnes,'" *Studies in Philology* 58 (1961), 533–55.

4. See my "*The Eve of St. Agnes* Reconsidered," *Tennessee Studies in Literature* 18 (1973), 113–32.

5. *The Letters of John Keats,* ed. Hyder E. Rollins (Cambridge, MA: Harvard UP, 1958), 2:223–24.

6. Ibid., 2:163.

7. On this idea in Western literature, see my *Reading T.S. Eliot: "Four Quartets" and the Journey toward Understanding* (New York: Palgrave Macmillan, 2012).

8. See T.S. Eliot, "Little Gidding," in *Four Quartets* (New York: Harcourt, Brace, 1943).

9. T.S. Eliot, *Ash-Wednesday: Six Poems (London: Faber and Faber, 1930).*

CHAPTER 5

"For Truth's Sake": "Lamia"
and the Reweaving of the Rainbow

Abstract "Lamia" is Keats's greatest success in representing ideas. Unlike his other poems, "Lamia," influenced by John Dryden and written in blank verse, explores dreams, reality, and the complex relations between them. It at once questions the possibility of (dramatized) "unperplexing" and separation and at the same time insists on the value and necessity of distinguishing. Close, extended attention to the famous passage on the "unweaving of a rainbow" reveals the complexity and sophistication of Keats's understanding and representation of philosophy and imagination; poetry, rather than philosophy, emerges as rational and critical, as well as imaginative and artful, Keats representing philosophy as within poetry instead of outside and governing it.

Keywords Ideas "unperplexing" · "rainbow" passage · Philosophy and imagination

> Do not all charms fly
> At the mere touch of cold philosophy?
> There was an awful rainbow once in heaven:
> We know her woof, her texture; she is given
> In the dull catalogue of common things.
> Philosophy will clip an angel's wings,
> Conquer all mysteries by rule and line,

© The Author(s) 2016
G.D. Atkins, *On Keats's Practice and Poetics of Responsibility*,
DOI 10.1007/978-3-319-44144-3_5

Empty the haunted air, and gnomed mine—
Unweave a rainbow, as it erewhile made
The tender-person'd Lamia felt into a shade.

—"Lamia"

forgetting the great end
Of poesy, that it should be a friend
To sooth the cares, and lift the thoughts of man.
. . . .
And they shall be accounted poet kings
Who simply tell the most heart-easing things.

—"Sleep and Poetry"

Can you imagine a greater contrast than that between "The Eve of St. Agnes" and "Lamia"? Poetically, I mean: John Dryden meets Edmund Spenser, heroic couplets in place of the luscious stanzaic form named for the Elizabethan poet? Thematically, some similarities exist, and we shall consider them in due course. But *contrast* surely strikes the reader both immediately and hardest. Of course, "contrast" also names the over-arching matter of Keats's last complete long poem.[1]

Perhaps the most obvious contrast is that between the Gods and men, intimated in these verses: "Real are the dreams of Gods, and smoothly pass/Their pleasures in a long immortal dream" (1.127–28). The contrast lies at the thematic heart of the poem, in which the responsible poet works even harder than in "The Eve of St. Agnes" to represent the perplexities surrounding the telling of truth and the human need of such consolations as beauty affords. At least much of the complexity that "Lamia" provides to the equation derives from the human need for reality, even in the midst of the most pleasing and tempting dreams.

I want to contextualize the contrast here between Gods and human-kind by means of a short discussion of the two *Hyperion* fragments, but first, I wish to return, more briefly still, to the "Ode to Psyche." The issue is the possibility of a new god, and that may helpfully be placed in the context of Roberto Calasso's important book *Literature and the Gods*.

As we recall, Psyche is first seen by the poet making love to "The winged boy." The poet laments that she came along too late to be revered as one of the Gods, "When holy were the haunted forest boughs,/Holy the air, the water, and the fire," the days of "happy pieties." Thus, Psyche has no "temple." The poet, though, will be Psyche's priest and "build a fane/In some untrodden region of *my mind*,/Where branched thoughts" will newly grow with "*pleasant pain*" (italics now added).

In Keats's poems, particularly "Lamia" and the two *Hyperion*s, the Gods are often out walking about. Are they literary furniture that Keats has appropriated, well aware that they have departed our world, or have they, as Ezra Pound believed, not returned because they never left? The question lies at the heart of *Literature and the Gods*, based on the Weidenfeld Lectures given the year before at Oxford University.

Among Calasso's many brilliant, and confident, claims is this, which perhaps directly recalls Keats on soul-making and the role of reading therein: "all the powers of the cult of the gods have migrated into a single, immobile and solitary act: that of reading."[2] Calasso gives special place to the Nymphs, whom he describes as "heralds of a form of knowledge, perhaps the most ancient, certainly the most dangerous: possession."[3] A manifestation of a power that has "split itself in two," the Nymph "is the *medium* in which gods and adventurous men may meet."[4] In the same breath, Calasso mentions Ezra Pound, the question being how can we recognize the gods: "No apter metaphor having been found for certain emotional colours," said Ole Ez, "I assert that the Gods exist," to which Calasso adds: "The writer is one who sees those 'emotional colours.'"[5]

Especially in the German Romantic poet Holderlin, Calasso locates a renewed sense of the divine as the "thing that imposes with maximum intensity the sensation of being alive. This is the immediate"—but, cautions Calasso, "pure intensity, as a continuous experience" (as revealed, I interject, in the fate of Lycius and Lamia), "is 'impossible,' overwhelming."[6] As to the Gods, Calasso quotes Mallarme: "'If the gods do nothing unseemly, then they are no longer gods at all.'"[7] It may well be that the goal is, and should be, "to overcome the discontinuous":

> to form something connected, something without a tear, or interruption, or break, through which the 'evil enemy' who is always ready to strike might creep in; something that, because of the elaborate nature of its composition, can stand up against the world, which presents itself to us as a series of 'isolated' ... entities. ... [8]

The essential point remains: "the gods manifest themselves above all as mental events."[9]

The Gods of "Lamia," especially Hermes—God of translation—with the nymph he loves (nymphs being associated, says Calasso, with interpretation), are presented, from the outset, as creatures of the long-gone past, thus the opening couplet: "Upon a time, before the faery broods/Drove Nymph and Satyr from the prosperous woods," whose story the poet will tell from the historical perspective. For context, consider that the two failed *Hyperion*'s—*Hyperion: A Fragment*, begun in the Fall of 1818 and abandoned in April of 1819, and *The Fall of Hyperion: A Dream*, on which Keats was working in the Fall of 1819—treat the eclipse of the Titans by the Gods, Saturn the center of attention in the first poem. A shift is noticeable in the later poem from the influence of Milton to that of Dante. Both poems, of course, evince a move from the luxurious stanzaic manner of earlier poems to blank verse. In *Hyperion: A Fragment*, Oceanus annunciates, speaking to Saturn, a psychological and spiritual position not at all out of line with Keats's own prevailing views but noteworthy in context: "How ye, perforce, must be content to stoop:/And in the proof much comfort will I give,/If ye will take that comfort in its truth." The "pain of truth" is, simply, pain, says Oceanus, referring to "Nature's law," "to bear all naked truths,/And to envisage circumstance, all calm,/That is the top of sovereignty" (2:178–81, 202–5).

From the start, *The Fall of Hyperion: A Dream* hunts big game, focusing on the power and place of "Poesy" and thus the imagination (along with dreaming). The opening verses set the stage: "Fanatics have their dreams, wherewith they weave/A paradise for a sect." Almost immediately we are told: "Poesy alone can tell her dreams,—/With the fine spell of words alone can save/Imagination from the sable chain/And dumb enchantment" (1.8–11). Moneta, one of the old Titans close to Saturn, offers solid advice to the poet who finds the old throne, distinguishing radically between the poet and the dreamer: "Only the dreamer," she says, "venoms all his days." The speaker she figures as "a dreaming thing,/A fever of thyself—think of the earth" (1.168–69). The poet, chimes in the speaker, is surely "a sage;/humanist, physician to all men./That I am none I feel" (1.189–91). Moneta then offers a moving account of the poet, in comparison with the dreamer: "The poet and the dreamer are distinct,/Diverse, sheer opposite, antipodes./The one pours out a balm upon the world,/The other vexes it." (1.199–202). We have here Keats's clearest, most direct statement of the character of the responsible poet.

"Lamia" opens, then, with a story of the Gods, at least of Hermes and his desire for a particular nymph; the snake-woman Lamia swears to help (perhaps recalling Angela) as long as Hermes, in turn, will provide assistance with her amorous desire for the young scholar-athlete Lycius, a mere mortal. Concerning the difference between the Gods and men, the narrator tells us: "Real are the dreams of Gods, and smoothly pass/Their pleasures in a long immortal dream" (1.127–28). "Mortal lovers" "grow pale," after all (1.145). The distinction hints at a dramatic contrast that the poem will pursue, between, that is, what is possible for men and what is not. It turns out to be a complicated—if not perplexing—story.

Of the serpent now turned back into fully woman, we read this description before Lycius encounters her, "happy Lycius" (1.185):

> A virgin purest lipp'd, yet in the lore
> Of love deep learn'd to the red heart's core:
> Not one hour old, yet of sciential brain
> To unperplex bliss from its neighbour pain;
> Define their pettish limits, and estrange
> Their points of contact, and swift counterchange;
> Intrigue with the specious chaos, and disport
> Its most ambiguous atoms with sure art.... (1.189–96)

That which is "unperplexed" from its opposite, here bliss and pain, we know, from "Ode to Psyche," for example, that Keats rejected. The word and the idea appear a bit later in "Lamia," for example, as every word the serpent "spake entic'd [Lycius] on/To unperplex'd delight and pleasure known" (1.326–27).

After the relatively brief account of Hermes and his desire for a Nymph, "Lamia" shifts to the serpent, whom Hermes transforms (back) into a woman. The story thereafter concerns (only) Lamia, Lycius, and his teacher, the philosopher Apollonius. She, of course, has long been smitten with the young Corinthian. At first, Lycius tells Lamia that she cannot ask him to remain "where no joy is,–/Empty of immortality and bliss." She responds that as "a scholar," "he must know/That finer spirits cannot breathe below/In human climes, and live" (1.277–81). She endeavors, upon his swooning, to reassure him, to "clear his soul of doubt," by playing the woman-card, claiming to be simply "a woman, and without/Any more subtle fluid in her veins/Than throbbing blood, and that the self-same pains/Inhabited her frail-strung heart as his" (1.305–9). Her words "entic'd him on/To unperplex'd delight and pleasure known" (1.326–27). Indeed, surmises the narrator: "Let the mad poets say whate'er they please/Of the sweets of Fairies, Peris, Goddesses,/There is nowhere such a treat/As a real woman, lineal indeed" (1.328–32).

In "half a fright," "gentle Lamia" realizes, Lycius "could not love." Reasoning correctly, she "threw the goddess off, and won his heart/More pleasantly by playing woman's part,/With no more awe than what her beauty gave,/That, while it smote, still guaranteed to save" (1.328–39). Matters get "perplexed," indeed, including the relation of the "real" and the "immortal." Of course, Lamia *plays* being a woman. Smiting is, we are told, also and at once saving.

Before being blinded by the erstwhile serpent, Lycius appears a good student of Apollonius—perhaps just a bit Wordsworthian, whether or not hinting at the "egotistical sublime." We first see Lycius as "Thoughtless," as "His phantasy was lost, where reason fades,/In the calm'd twilight of Platonic shades." Indeed, he was "shut up in mysteries,/His mind wrapp'd up like his mantle. . . . " (1.233–42). Fantasy and thoughtlessness are thus represented as the opposite of another quality or qualities that the poem proceeds to explore.

This account of what philosophy has done to Lycius's mind, shutting it and wrapping it up, prepares us for meeting his teacher, Apollonius, whom Lycius shrinks from encountering and whom Lamia fears from the start: "'Tis Apollonius sage, my trusty guide/And good instructor; but to-night he seems/The ghost of folly haunting my sweet dreams" (1.375–77). Dreams and reality are (further) perplexed: Lycius would, though, keep them entirely separate from one another.

The narrator, meanwhile, asserts his primary responsibility to truth. Acknowledging his reader's likely desire, he does not buy into the half-truth that would "leave them thus." He does not care to "humour his reader," just as at the end of "The Eve of St. Agnes," the narrator there refuses to leave Madeline and Porphyro, in the words of the later poem, "Shut from the busy world of more incredulous" (1.394–7). Thus ends Part I of "Lamia," on the note of care and concern for the reader that we saw in "The Eve of St. Agnes," where its door, groaning, opens mysteriously onto a world hardly better, probably, than that the door had kept out.

Part II actually takes off from just this ending of the first part, extending the noted concern and elaborating on it in a way that all the more perplexes: "Love in a hut, with water and a crust,/Is—Love, forgive us!—cinders, ashes, dust;/ Love in a palace is perhaps at last/ More grievous torment than a hermit's fast" (2.1–4). The narrator immediately adds: "That is a doubtful tale from faery land,/Hard for the non-elect to understand" (2.5–6).

The plot resumes, with a twist. After making love one "even tide," the happy couple are resting, "side by side," when suddenly, from the outside, sounds erupt: specifically, "a thrill/Of trumpets," at which Lycius "started." Though the sounds quickly "fled," they "left a thought, a buzzing in his head." And that eventually proves fatal, literally: "For the first time, since first [Lycius] harbour'd in/That purple-lined palace of sweet sin,/His spirit pass'd beyond its golden bourn/Into the noisy world almost forsworn." The narrator's following words emphasize Lamia's powers of observation and her skills at reading—she is described here as "ever watchful, penetrant." *What* she sees, makes all the difference in the world, for Lycius's wandering imaginative eye points, she immediately recognizes, to a lack or absence, "a want/of something more than her empery/Of joys." The "want" is, of course, not really a failure on Lamia's part. The problem lies, rather, in the unbridgeable difference between these represented "worlds" or dimensions. Upon such reflection, Lamia "began to moan and sigh/Because he mused beyond her, knowing well/That but a moment's thought is passion's passing bell" (2.16–39). Especially given the poem's emphasis on the repeated warnings not to "unperplex" bliss and pain, this does not bode well: Lycius precisely finds the utter separation of bliss and pain, passion and thought, isolation and engagement, unsatisfying, insufficient. He needs more; he needs *other*.

Lycius's "want" is not altogether praiseworthy; indeed, it is, even if understandable, selfish, vain, and egotistical; Lycius desires the envy of friend and foe alike. The philosophically trained young man turns Lamia's perhaps surprisingly philosophical and specifically metaphysical analysis into a homelier psychological and moral consideration, but his reflection precisely acts as a dramatic monologue does, revealing more and other than he intends: "What mortal hath a prize, that other men/May be confounded and abash'd withal,/But lets it sometimes pace abroad majes-tical,/And triumph" (2.57–60). Thus Lycius continues, his ego plainly gaining the upper hand, his *desire* triumphant: "Amid the hoarse alarm of Corinth's voice" "Let my foes choke, and my friends shout afar,/While through the thronged streets your bridal car/Wheels round its dazzling spokes" (2.61–64)

As it was the Corinthian custom then to "bring away/The bride from home at blushing shut of day" (2.106–7), a great feast is prepared. Lamia has beseeched Lycius to keep her hidden from the philosopher, old Apollonius. The day arrives, and the narrator utters these warnings to Lycius, confirming the foolishness of Lycius's proud desire to parade his most beautiful bride: "O senseless Lycius! Madman! wherefore flout/The silent-blessing fate, warm cloister'd hours,/And show to common eyes these secret bowers?" (2.147–49). And, lo and behold, there is Apollonius: "something too he laugh'd,/As though some knotty problem, that had daft/His patient thought, had now begun to thaw,/And solve and melt:—'twas just as he foresaw" (2.159–62).

In meeting his "young disciple," Apollonius admits that it was "wrong" to crash the party, but then he adds, attesting to his felt sense of responsibility for his student: "yet must I do this wrong/And you forgive me" (2.168–69). At this, "Lycius blush'd, and led/The old man through the inner doors broad-spread;/With reconciling words and courteous mien/ Turning into sweet milk the sophist's spleen" (2.169–72). Lycius seems pusillanimous and hardly willing to defend either his own actions or Lamia.

The narrator is different. Indeed, in the most famous passage in the poem, he finds all three central dramatis personae at fault—and moves out into strong denunciations of such philosophy as Apollonius practices and evidently embodies. The passage deserves quoting in full.

> What wreath for Lamia? What for Lycius?
> What for the sage, old Apollonius?
> Upon her aching forehead be there hung
> The leaves of willow and of adder's tongue;
> And for the youth, quick, let us strip for him
> The thyrsus, that his watching eyes may swim
> Into forgetfulness; and, for the sage,
> Let spear-grass and the spiteful thistle wage
> War on his temples. (2.221–29)

The linguistic register here is "poetic," flowery, and Romantic, but the organization is very different. It is ratiocinative. Together, these elements accentuate the doubleness and complexity that is "Lamia."

At this point, the verse paragraph turns, modulating, outward to cultural reflection and criticism:

> Do not all charms fly
> At the mere touch of cold philosophy?
> There was an awful rainbow once in heaven:
> We know her woof, her texture; she is given
> In the dull catalogue of common things.

> Philosophy will clip an angel's wings,
> Conquer all mysteries by rule and line,
> Empty the haunted air, and gnomed mine—
> Unweave a rainbow, as it erewhile made
> The tender-person'd Lamia melt into a shade. (2.229–38)

This statement of ideas essentially completes the story, although details will be later, and briefly, represented. The ideas thus highlighted, action recedes into the background, and if we did not know before, we know now that Keats is no "versifying pet-lamb."

Keats's voice here is, to say the least, impressive: assured, balanced, thematically responsible in linking unmistakably what has happened thanks to "philosophy" and what happens to Lamia (and as a consequence, Lycius, too). Reflecting the influence of John Dryden, whom Keats had been reading, the heroic couplet seems right for this truth-telling, which, here, derives not from observation but from reasoned interpretation. It seems, as a matter of fact, that the voice we hear in these magnificent, right-minded lines is Truth itself.

The end is then detailed in somewhat over 50 remaining verses. It contains no surprises. Lycius had intended to "pledge" his old teacher, but "The bald-head philosopher/Had fix'd his eye, without a twinkle or stir/Full on the alarmed beauty of the bride,/Brow-beating her fair form, and troubling her sweet pride" (2.205–8). In response to his cold, stony gaze, Lamia's hand grows "icy," and immediately "the cold ran through [Lycius's] veins" (2.251). Lycius responds then to Apollonius, blaming him alone for everything now happening. His old teacher replies, in turn: "'Fool!' said the sophist, in an under-tone/Gruff with contempt; which a death-nighing moan/From Lycius answer'd, as heart-struck and lost/He sank supine beside the aching ghost" (2.291–94). "'Fool! Fool!'" repeated he, while his eyes still/Relented not, nor mov'd; 'from every ill /Of life have I preserv'd thee to this day,/And shall I see thee made a serpent's prey?'" (2.295–98)

Little remains to be said, as the story moves to conclusion, and the poem:

> Then Lamia breath'd death breath; the sophist's eye,
> Like a sharp spear, went through her utterly,
> Keen, cruel, perceant, stinging: she, as well
> As her weak hand could any meaning tell,
> Motion'd him to be silent; vainly so,

He look'd and look'd again a level—No!
"A Serpent!" echoed he; no sooner said,
Than with a frightful scream she vanished:
And Lycius's arms were empty of delight,
As were his limbs of life, from that same night.
On the high couch he lay!—his friends came round—
Supported him—no pulse, or breath they found,
And in its marriage robe, the heavy body wound. (2.299–311)

Coming away from "Lamia," we recognize that we have been in the presence of a complex—and complex-ifying—poem, quite likely a great one.[10] I have said before that it is a poem of ideas, and I want to return to and develop that point. In order to do so efficiently, let us look again at the imaginative passage on "philosophy" and its capacity to "unweave a rainbow."

The passage is not dramatic, but straightforward. It carries the ring of a choral statement. The verses are spoken by the narrator, but, as I said above, they are likely to convince us that they bear the burden of Truth itself. Does anything in the poem question them, or does everything support them? We may not much care for, or agree completely with, what they say. At any rate, they open, undogmatically, with a question, albeit a rhetorical one, and end by returning to the specifics of the rather simple plot, the entailed ideas thus framed, and spotlighted.

The passage carries, as I say, the heft of Truth. I am not sure, however, that that Truth feels earned. Moreover, its applicability may not be unproblematic—in light of the extenuating circumstances surrounding the favored, and anti-Apollonian, points of view of both Lamia and Lycius. Much depends, of course, on the character and reliability of the narrator, who does not hesitate to express his opinion throughout the poem; he is not a part of the plot, having no ostensible role in it, albeit he is not loathe to address the characters. The "human" characters, furthermore, Lycius, Lamia (if we can call her that), and Apollonius, by no means seem realistic, even if their actions are explicable in terms of human psychology. They come to Keats's pages from the depths of myth, and because they do, it may be that we are not inclined to care about them as personae as such. In this poem, moreover, it is what the characters stand for as ideas that really matters. Apollonius represents philosophy, and the narrator is unsympathetic toward him, in line with the declaration-as-truth in the passage regarding the unweaving of a rainbow.

With the annunciations in this passage, we find confirmation of what the entire poem reveals: Truth and Beauty are *unperplexed*, separated from one another. In "Lamia," truth is not beautiful, nor is beauty truth. The beautiful, passionate world, admittedly artificial and contrived by the serpent, is not enough for Lycius. The poem says it directly, affirming Lamia's own perception: her lover's "spirit pass'd beyond its golden bourn/Into the noisy world *almost* forsworn" (italics now added), "arguing a want/Of something more, more than her empery/Of joys" (2.32–33). The truth is, of course, although the poem does not quite say it, that Lycius passes "beyond" the "bourn" of reality in blinding himself regarding both Lamia and her "creations." Lamia *is* a serpent, pretending to be a real woman, and the "place" she makes for the occasion is a feat of God-like magic; it does not represent another dimension intersecting with our mundane world and everyday life. It cannot last, or, rather, as just observed, it is not enough for a human being. The "more" needed is reality, including a real woman.

In this regard, "Lamia" may remind you of T.S. Eliot's *Animula*, on which I have commented in the second chapter above, and another of his Ariel or Christmas poems, this one in the new series *The Cultivation of Christmas Trees*.[11] The first of these poems, as we have seen, embraces the child's, and the child-like's, "confounding" of the real and the imagined and imaginary. In various poems and essays, Eliot extolled the "necessarye coniunction" and the "impossible union" of apparent opposites, such as, to take Keatsian "oppositions," pleasure or bliss and melancholy.[12] Neither poet would separate these differences. But Keats was adamant, as we are seeing, that the dream-world not be confused with the real. Eliot, though, in the 1954 Ariel poem, again evoked, and embraced, the child-like, "For whom the candle is a star, and the gilded angel/Spreading its wings at the summit of the tree/*Is not only a decoration, but an angel*" (italics added).[13] For Eliot, (at least) two dimensions "exist," the "other" dimension "attending" this one. Keats, on the other hand, writes, not of two dimensions, but of two quite different realities, one of which is simply mysterious, a creation of a god, perhaps, indeed, a dream.

In several ways, therefore, "Lamia," a late poem, complicates Keats's habit of complex-ifying. Truth-telling is not a simple polar opposition to dreaming, as other poems might lead us to believe. Things are more complicated, and "circumstances" rear their heads, ugly or not. In other words, the situation is, indeed, *perplexed*. "Lamia" succeeds certainly to this extent: it refuses to accept any truth less or other than that which includes as part of its truth the truth that truth-telling sometimes (at least) results in destruction. In that sense, too, then, the poem (further) separates beauty from truth.

"Lamia" must, in the final analysis, be said to confirm what the structure reveals in functioning: the Gods and men are themselves "unperplexed" and separate. This may well be one of the truths that Keats is so concerned to show, thus "soothing" us and "lifting our thoughts." Extrapolating from our discussion, we might conclude that the poem is like the rainbow: thematically speaking, that is, for it represents the way beauty is "unwoven" by philosophy. But then, meta-critically (as it were), the very act of close-reading the poem, along the lines followed in these pages, unweaves some (at least) of the magic that the poem comprises absent knowing its "woof" and its "texture."

"Lamia" is clearly a complex effort at complexi-fying; it is Keats's greatest poem of ideas. The poem may be *perplexing*, as well as perplexed. If that is so, and I think it is, what, then, of its capacity for soothing and lifting our thoughts? The passage on philosophy and its effects on our perception of beauty stands out, in any case. In part, that distinctive quality derives from its actual difference from the rest of the poem. That is, it unquestionably lambastes philosophy, and by extension Apollonius, but the rest of "Lamia" has less to do with the philosophy and the point of view Apollonius holds than with other ideas, notably including the relation of Gods and men, the seductiveness of unperplexed pleasure and pain, joy and melancholy, the incapacity of anything but the real to hold our interest and provide satisfaction. Lamia's beauty "smites" (as Apollonius understands), but the narrator says it is also "guaranteed to save." As the narrator further, and accordingly, avers, "'Twould humour many a heart to leave" Lycius and Lamia alone, "Shut from the busy world of more incredulous." But as always with Keats, "the flitter-winged verse must tell,/For truth's sake, what woe afterwards befel" (1.394–97).

Keats does not simply attack philosophy and analytical reasoning (as much as he embraced what he called in a letter "negative capability").[14] Nor does he simply embrace and endorse imagination, or dreaming. "Lamia" is much too complex to juxtapose reason with imagination, call them opposites, and have done with it. A host of problems lie with the anti-philosophy "side." And of course, at least implicitly, the very idea and function of "side"—that is, part-ial thinking—is an important part of the poem's interest.

Let us linger just a bit longer with these verses. Consider most simply, that is literally, that the poem (as a whole) *incorporates* that verse paragraph. That fact does not fail to carry meaning and significance.

Rather than a "choral statement" as I have ventured above, these verses on the unweaving of the rainbow at the hands of philosophy and analytic reasoning are properly seen, not quite as dramatic, but as participants in a whole that, while encompassing them, yet reveals a relation of tension with other parts. It is the case that the poem "Lamia" seen as a whole disparages and denounces philosophy in philosophical terms.

But not unrelievably philosophical, or simply analytic. The passage is beautifully figurative and imaginative, flanked with rhetorical questions, as well as sympathy and compassion for the supposedly anti-philosophy figure of the serpent Lamia herself. The upshot is that we come away agreeing with Horatio in *Hamlet* that there is more involved in the world than philosophy (alone) ever dreamed of. Meditating on the verses just a bit more, we realize that "Lamia" dramatizes just how the imagination, and the work of poetry rather than philosophy, is effectively reasonable and critical. (The even younger Alexander Pope had said it in *An Essay on Criticism* in 1711: wit carries judgment within itself.)[15] Reason is no more satisfactory when separate than the magically created world that cannot long hold Lycius's attention, one from which he must inevitably return to the real world of the quotidian and the "perplexed" and perplexing.

Furthermore, the relation uncovered between lines 221–38 and the rest of "Lamia" leads us to question the absolute statement that I rendered earlier concerning the poem as centrally interested in ideas. The "truthful" paragraph on Apollonius, philosophy, and the unweaving of the rainbow presents ideas disembodied, whereas the remainder of the poem, the more imaginative and "literary" parts, treats ideas as embodied in characters, even if those figures are hardly rounded or capable of being mistaken as "real" beyond the poem.

"Lamia" offers a world in which the Gods once existed—and to which they have returned by means of Keats's poem. The suggestion seems clear: the rainbow, too, still exists, even if it has been un-woven by philosophic reasoning. We are called (back) to the rainbow, just as Lycius is to the ordinary world of Corinth. We may have to re-imagine things, perhaps ourselves return with and in difference. Who knows, moreover? The Gods and men can mix, although they cannot live together, not for very long, at least.[16]

The great Modernist poet, who repudiated Romantic reflection and lyrical self-expression, devoted his first book of critical essays to ideas, their place in poetry, and ways of integrating them into poetry (*The Sacred Wood: Essays on Poetry and Criticism,* 1920). T.S. Eliot was trained, at Harvard, as a philosopher, and indeed completed all work for a Ph.D. except the defense of his dissertation, which was eventually published (in 1964, as *Knowledge and Experience in the Philosophy of F.H. Bradley*). To compare Keats with Eliot in terms of the ideas in their poems may arouse cries of invidiousness. After all, the Victorians thought Keats painted pretty pictures, but was sorely lacking in ideas (the charge sometimes brought against other Romantics as well). In the preceding pages, I have presented a different picture of Keats, beginning with the significant ideas confronted and sometimes challenged in the Letters and proceeding with the fact that several of the great Odes take as their overt subjects such ideas as indolence, melancholy, and autumn; the fact that "The Eve of St. Agnes" embeds ideas concerning the Christian religion as well as possibilities for earthly happiness in, for example, the imaginative and artful frame surrounding the story of hardly naturalistic "characters"; and, finally, as we have just seen, the highly sophisticated treatment of philosophy, imagination, and poetry in the complex and complex-ifying verse of "Lamia."

Rather than minimizing Keats's importance, or his stature, comparison with Eliot actually works to Keats's benefit, for reading the older poet alongside the younger presents both new avenues into Keats's poetry and fresh subjects for consideration. While I certainly do not claim philosophical sophistication for Keats, I believe I have shown that, far from a poet uninterested in ideas or incapable of integrating them into his poetry and responding capaciously to them, he was able to see and to dramatize a fruitful understanding of the relation of, for instance, philosophy and imagination.

Keats was no "egotistical sublime"; his verse is not about himself, his dreams, or his ideas. He neither "expresses" his own feelings, nor engages in reflection, which signals a gap in time following "experience." The poetry is observational, dramatic, and "objective." In the great Ode, Keats not only *embodies* Autumn, but he also works within language to allow a new sense, a new idea and understanding, of the season quietly to emerge.

"Lamia" may be said to extend this recognition, and to expand upon this achievement. Keats directly challenges the place and power of philosophy and does so with balance, judgment, and intelligence born not of abstract reasoning but of imagination and artistic acumen leavened with good sense. In the end, he understands, and shows, that philosophy does not come to poetry from outside it with ideas ready for expression but, instead, emerges from within language and what Eliot calls the "intolerable wrestle" of the poet with words.

NOTES

1. On Keats's signifying use of contrast, see note 1 in Chapter 4 above.
2. Roberto Calasso, *Literature and the Gods* (New York: Knopf, 2001), 22.
3. Ibid., 30.
4. Ibid., 33.
5. Ibid., 33–34.
6. Ibid., 39.
7. Ibid., 104.
8. Ibid., 160.
9. Ibid., 169. Keats could be profitably compared and contrasted with Pound on the matters of the Gods. An inveterate enemy of established churches (which he described as "an outrage") and of dogma (which he called "bluff based upon ignorance"), Pound insisted that "the essence of religion is the *present* tense," and in "Religio or, The Child's Guide to Knowledge," he offered the following description of the Gods:

What is a god?
A god is an eternal state of mind.
What is a faun?
A faun is an elemental creature.
What is a nymph?
A nymph is an elemental creature.
When is a god manifest?
When the states of mind take form.
When does a man become a god?
When he enters one of these states of mind.
What is the nature of the forms whereby a god is manifest?
They are variable but retain certain distinguishing characteristics.
Are all eternal states of mind gods?
We consider them so to be.
Are all durable states of mind gods?
They are not.
By what characteristics may we know the divine forms?
By beauty.

And if the presented forms are unbeautiful?
They are demons. . . .

Quoted from Ezra Pound, *Selected Prose, 1909–1965,* ed. William Cookson
(New York: New Directions, 1975), 410, 49, 43, 47.

10. An apposite, little-considered poem, is Ode ['Bards of Passion'], written in
late 1818 in a copy of Beaumont and Fletcher's *The Fair Maid of the Inn* and
copied by Keats into a letter of December 1818–January 1819 to his brother
and sister-in-law, George and Georgiana. I quote it here—I do not pretend
that the diction is sharp or always successful, nor the rhymes always effective,
but the themes treated shed some light, I believe, on the complexity of
"Lamia."

Bards of Passion and of Mirth,
Ye have left your souls on earth!
Have ye souls in heaven too,
Double-lived in regions new?
Yes, and those of heaven commune
With the spheres of sun and moon;
With the noise of fountains wond'rous,
And the parle of voices thund'rous;
With the whisper of heaven's trees
And one another, in soft ease
Seated on Elysian lawns
Brows'd by none but Dian's fawns;
Underneath large blue-bells tented,
Where the daisies are rose-scented,
And the rose herself has got
Perfume which on earth is not;
Where the nightingale doth sing
Not a senseless, tranced thing,
But divine, melodious truth;
Philosophic numbers smooth;
Tales and golden histories
Of heaven and its mysteries.

Thus ye live on high, and then
On the earth ye live again;
And the souls ye left behind you
Teach us, here, the way to find you,
Where your other souls are joying,
Never slumber'd, never cloying.
Here, your earth-born souls still speak

To mortals, of their little week;
Of their sorrows and delights;
Of their passions and their spites;
Of their glory and their shame;
What doth strengthen and what maim.
Thus ye teach us, every day,
Wisdom, though fled far away.
    Bards of Passion and of Mirth,
Ye have left your souls on earth!
Ye have souls in heaven too,
Double-lived in regions new!

There is a doubleness here, not so much a complexi-fying or "perplexing." In the letter to George and Georgiana, John Keats locates the theme in "the double immortality of Poets." The quality of the poetry belies the serious-ness of the ideas. The "Bards of Passion and of Mirth" have *souls made.* (Keats *Selected Poems and Letters*, ed. Douglas Bush (Boston, MA: Riverside-Houghton Mifflin, 1959), 261.

11. T.S. Eliot, *Animula* (London: Faber and Faber, 1929); and *The Cultivation of Christmas Trees* (London: Faber and Faber, 1954).
12. T.S. Eliot, *Four Quartets* (New York: Harcourt, Brace, 1943).
13. See also my *T.S. Eliot's Christmas Poems: An Essay in Writing-as-Reading and Other "Impossible Unions"* (New York: Palgrave Macmillan, 2014).
14. Keats, *Selected Poems and Letters*, 261.
15. Alexander Pope, *An Essay on Criticism,* in *Poetry and Prose,* ed. Aubrey Williams (Boston, MA: Riverside-Houghton Mifflin, 1969).
16. At the end of "Lamia," Keats added as a note a quotation from Burton's *Anatomy of Melancholy,* in which appears a story of Lycius and Apollonius that he largely follows. Clearly, Keats changed the thematic focus—but includ-ing the quotation does nothing to diminish the fictive nature of the poem, enhanced, of course, by, among other new features, the opening that Keats added regarding the god Hermes:

Philostratus, in his fourth book *de Vita Apollonii,* hath a memorable instance in this kind, which I may not omit, of one Menippus Lycius, a young man twenty-five years of age, that going betwixt Cenchreas and Corinth, met such a phantasm in the habit of a fair gentlewoman, which taking him by the hand, carried him home to her house, in the suburbs of Corinth, and told him she was a Phoenician by birth, and if he would tarry with her, he should hear her sing and play, and drink such wine as never any drank, and no man should molest him; but she, being fair and lovely, would live and die with him, that was fair and lovely to behold.

The young man, a philosopher, otherwise staid and discreet, able to
moderate his passions, though not this of love, tarried with him a while
to his great content, and at last married her, to whose wedding, amongst
other guests, came Apollonius, who, by some probable conjectures,
found her out to be a serpent, a lamia; and that all her furniture was,
like Tantalus' gold, described by Homer, no substance but mere illusions. When she saw herself descried, she wept, and desired Apollonius to
be silent, but he would not be moved, and thereupon she, plate, house,
and all that was in it, vanished in an instant: many thousands took notice
of this fact, for it was done in the midst of Greece. In *Selected Poems and
Letters* 228 [From Part 3 Sect. 2 Memb. 1 Subs. 1].

BIBLIOGRAPHY

Abrams, M.H. *Natural Supernaturalism: Tradition and Revolution in Romantic Literature.* New York: Norton, 1971.

Atkins, G. Douglas. "A(fter) D(econstruction): Literature and Religion in the Wake of Deconstruction," *Studies in the Literary Imagination* 18 (1985), 89–100.

Atkins, G. Douglas. "Dehellenizing Literary Criticism." *College English* 41 (1980), 769–79.

Atkins, G. Douglas. "Dryden's *Religio Laici*: A Reappraisal." *Studies in Philology* 75 (1978), 347–70.

Atkins, G. Douglas. "*The Eve of St. Agnes* Reconsidered." *Tennessee Studies in Literature* 18 (1973), 113–32.

Atkins, G. Douglas. "'A Grander Scheme of Salvation than the Chryst[e]ain Religion': John Keats, a New Religion of Love, and the Hoodwinking of 'The Eve of St. Agnes,'" *Literary Paths to Religious Understanding: Essays on Dryden, Pope, Keats, George Eliot, Joyce, T.S. Eliot, and E.B. White.* New York: Palgrave Macmillan, 2009, 43–57.

Atkins, G. Douglas. *On the Familiar Essay: Challenging Academic Orthodoxies.* New York: Palgrave Macmillan, 2009.

Atkins, G. Douglas *Reading Essays: An Invitation.* Athens: U of Georgia P, 2008.

Atkins, G. Douglas. *Tracing the Essay: Through Experience to Meaning.* Athens: U of Georgia P, 2005.

Atkins, G. Douglas. *T.S. Eliot's Christmas Poems: An Essay in Writing-as-Reading and Other "Impossible Unions."* New York: Palgrave Macmillan, 2014.

Attridge, Derek. *Reading and Responsibility: Deconstruction's Traces.* Edinburgh: Edinburgh UP, 2010.

Baldwin, James. *Notes of a Native Son.* Boston, MA: Beacon Press, 1955.

© The Author(s) 2016
G.D. Atkins, *On Keats's Practice and Poetics of Responsibility*,
DOI 10.1007/978-3-319-44144-3

Benziger, James. *Images of Eternity: Studies in the Poetry of Religious Vision from Wordsworth to T.S. Eliot*. Carbondale: Southern Illinois UP, 1962.

Bewell, Alan. "'To Autumn' and the Curing of Space." In Cox, Ed. *Poetry and Prose of John Keats*, 634–42.

Bostetter, Edward E. "The Eagle and the Truth: Keats and the Problem of Belief." *Journal of Aesthetics and Art Criticism* 16 (1958): 362–72.

Boulger, James D. "Keats' Symbolism." *ELH* 28 (1961): 244–59.

Bush, Douglas. "Keats and His Ideas." In *The Major English Romantic Poets: A Symposium in Reappraisal*, ed. Clarence D. Thorpe, Carlos Baker, and Bennett Weaver. Carbondale: Southern Illinois UP. 231–45.

Cox, Jeffrey N., Ed. *Poetry and Prose of John Keats*. Norton Critical Editions. New York: Norton, 2008.

Davis, Walter A. *The Act of Interpretation: A Critique of Literary Reason*. Chicago, IL: U of Chicago P, 1978.

Detweiler, Robert, and David Jasper, Eds. *Religion and Literature: A Reader*. Louisville, KY: Westminster-John Knox, 2000.

Eliot, T.S. *Animula*. London: Faber and Faber, 1929.

Eliot, T.S. *Ash-Wednesday: Six Poems*. London: Faber and Faber, 1930.

Eliot, T.S. *Collected Poems 1909–1962*. New York: Harcourt, Brace, 1991.

Eliot, T.S. *The Cultivation of Christmas Trees*. London: Faber and Faber, 1954.

Eliot, T.S. *Essays Ancient and Modern*. London: Faber and Faber, 1936.

Eliot, T.S. *Four Quartets*. New York: Harcourt, Brace, 1943.

Eliot, T.S. "Religion and Literature." *Selected Essays*. 388–401.

Eliot, T.S. *The Sacred Wood: Essays on Poetry and Criticism*. London: Methuen, 1920.

Eliot, T.S. *Selected Essays*. 3rd. ed. London: Faber and Faber, 1951.

Fitzgerald, F. Scott. *The Crack-Up*. Ed. Edmund Wilson. New York: New Directions, 1945.

Ford, Newell F. "Holy Living and Holy Dying in Keats's Poetry." *Keats-Shelley Journal* 20 (1971): 37–61.

Fraistat, Neil. "'Lamia' Progressing: Keats's Volume." In Cox, Ed. *Poetry and Prose of John Keats*. 592–604.

Fry, Paul H. *The Reach of Criticism: Method and Perception in Literary Theory*. New Haven, CT: Yale UP, 1983.

Gardner, Helen. *Religion and Literature*. London: Faber and Faber, 1971.

Gigante, Denise. *The Keats Brothers: The Life of John and George*. Cambridge, MA: Belknap P of Harvard UP, 2013.

Gittings, Robert. *John Keats*. London: Heinemann, 1968.

Hartman, Geoffrey H. *Criticism in the Wilderness: The Study of Literature Today*. New Haven, CT: Yale UP, 1980.

Holderness, Graham. *Tales from Shakespeare: Creative Collisions*. Cambridge: Cambridge UP, 2014.

Joyce, James. *A Portrait of the Artist as a Young Man*. Ed. Chester G. Anderson. 1916. New York: Viking-Penguin, 1964.

Keats, John. *Complete Poems*. Ed. Jack Stillinger. Cambridge, MA: Belknap P of Harvard UP, 1978.

Keats, John. *The Letters of John Keats*. Ed. Hyder E. Rollins. 2 vols. Cambridge, MA: Harvard UP, 1958.

Keats, John. *Selected Poems and Letters*. Ed. Douglas Bush. Boston, MA: Riverside-Houghton Mifflin, 1959.

Keats, John. *The Letters of John Keats*. Ed. Grant Scott. Cambridge, MA: Harvard UP, 2005.

Keats, John. *Poetical Works*. Ed. H.W. Garrod. 1956. London: Oxford UP, 1966.

Keats, John. *Poetry and Prose*. Ed. Jeffrey N. Cox. Norton Critical Editions. New York: Norton, 2008.

Knight, G. Wilson. "The Priest-like Task: An Essay on Keats." In *The Starlit Dome: Studies in the Poetry of Vision*. London: Oxford UP, 1941. 258–307.

Lytle, Andrew. *The Hero with the Private Parts*. Baton Rouge: Louisiana State UP, 1966.

Miller, Hugh. *Essays*. vol. 1. London, 1856.

Miller, J. Hillis. "Literature and Religion." In *Relations of Literary Study: Essays on Interdisciplinary Contributions*. Ed. James Thorpe. New York: MLA. 111–26.

Motion, Andrew. *Keats*. New York: Farrar, Straus and Giroux, 1998.

Plumly, Stanley. *Posthumous Keats: A Personal Biography*. New York: Norton, 2009.

Pope, Alexander. *Poetry and Prose*. Ed. Aubrey Williams. Boston, MA: Riverside-Houghton Mifflin, 1969.

Pound, Ezra. *ABC of Reading*. London: Routledge, 1934.

Pound, Ezra. *Selected Prose, 1909–1965*. Ed. William Cookson. New York: New Directions, 1975.

Roe, Nicholas. *John Keats: A New Life*. New Haven, CT: Yale UP, 2012.

Rossetti, William Michael. *Life of John Keats*. London, 1887.

Ryan, Robert M. *Keats: The Religious Sense*. Princeton, NJ: Princeton UP, 1976.

Schneidau, Herbert N. *Sacred Discontent: The Bible and Western Tradition*. Baton Rouge: Louisiana State UP, 1976.

Scott, Grant. "Keats in His Letters." In Cox, Ed. *Poetry and Prose of John Keats*. 555–63.

Sharp, Ronald A. *Keats, Skepticism, and the Religion of Beauty*. Athens: U of Georgia P, 1979.

Sisson, C.H. *The Avoidance of Literature: Collected Essays*. Manchester: Carcanet, 1978.

Sperry, Stuart M., Jr. "Romance as Wish-Fulfillment: Keats's *The Eve of St. Agnes*." *Studies in Romanticism* 10 (1971): 27–42.

Stillinger, Jack. "The Hoodwinking of Madeline: Scepticism in 'The Eve of St. Agnes.'" *Studies in Philology* 58 (1961): 533–55.

Stillinger, Jack. *"The Hoodwinking of Madeline" and Other Essays on Keats's Poems.* Urbana: U of Illinois P, 1971.

Stillinger, Jack. *Reading "The Eve of St. Agnes": The Multiples of Complex Literary Transaction.* Oxford: Oxford UP, 1999.

Waldoff, Leon. "From Abandonment to Scepticism in Keats." *Essays in Criticism.* 21 (1971): 152–58.

Ward, Aileen. *John Keats: The Making of a Poet.* New York: Viking, 1963.

Wasserman, Earl. *The Finer Tone: Keats' Major Poems.* Baltimore: Johns Hopkins P, 1953.

White, E.B. *Essays.* New York: Harper & Row, 1977.

White, R.S. *John Keats: A Literary Life.* Basingstoke: Palgrave Macmillan, 2010.

Williams, Rowan. *Grace and Necessity: Reflections on Art and Love.* Harrisburg, PA: Morehouse, 2005.

Wolfson. Susan J., Ed. *Cambridge Companion to John Keats.* Cambridge: Cambridge UP, 2001.

Wolfson. Susan J., Ed. *Reading John Keats.* Cambridge: Cambridge UP, 2015.

Woodhouse, A.S.P. *The Poet and His Faith: Religion and Poetry in England from Spenser to Eliot and Auden.* Chicago, IL: U of Chicago P, 1965.

Wordsworth, William. Preface to *Lyrical Ballads.* In *The Norton Anthology of English Literature*, 6th edn, ed. M.H. Abrams et al. vol. 22. New York: Norton, 1993. 141–52.

Wordsworth, William. *The Prelude.* In *The Norton Anthology.*

Yost, George, Jr. "Keats's Early Religious Phraseology." *Studies in Philology* 59 (1962): 579–91.

INDEX

A

Abide and embrace two conflicting
ideas at once, 24
Adonais, 11
Andrewes, Lancelot, 34
Anglo-Catholic Christianity,
34, 38
Animula, 21, 22,
41, 77
Annus mirabilis, 63
Another dimension, 64
Anti-Christian, 54
Apuleius, 39
Ariel or Christmas poem, 41, 77
Aristotelian rather than Platonic, 22
Asceticism, 54, 56
Ash-Wednesday, 23,
38, 63
Audience, 7, 8

B

Bailey, Benjamin, 13,
14, 26
Baldwin, James, 24
Barthes, Roland, 4
Bate, Walter Jackson, 7, 40
Beauty and its relation to truth, 26

Beauty that Keats interested in as
inseparable from the truth told in
and by the representation, 48
Beauty & Truth, 27, 28
Between conception and expression, 37
Between Gods and humankind, 68, 71
Between the poet and the dreamer, 70
Biblical, 46, 63, 65
Binary opposite, 18
Binds us to the earth, 65
Blackwood's Edinburgh Magazine, 11
Blank verse, 70
Bloom, Harold, 5
Brawne, Fanny, 10, 60
Brothers George and Thomas, 24
Browning, Robert, 44
Burden of Truth itself, 76
"Burnt, Norton", 46, 47, 65
Bush, Douglas, 23, 29

C

Calasso, Roberto, 68
Care and concern for the reader, 72
Change, 37, 47, 52, 58, 61, 64
Character as such, in the Odes, and
even in "The Eve of St. Agnes",
matters little, 35

© The Author(s) 2016
G.D. Atkins, *On Keats's Practice and Poetics of Responsibility*,
DOI 10.1007/978-3-319-44144-3

Printed in Great Britain
by Amazon

40949717R00066